JOURNEY THROUGH SOUTHERN INDIA

JOURNEY THROUGH SOUTHERN INDIA

MARK PROBERT

First published in the UK in January 2025 by Journey Books, an imprint of Bradt Travel Guides Ltd 31a High Street, Chesham, Buckinghamshire, HP5 1BW, England
www.bradtguides.com

Text copyright © 2025 Mark Probert
Edited by Jill Sawyer

Cover illustration and design by Thomas Probert
Photographs copyright © Individual photographers, 2025 (see below)
Layout and typesetting by Ian Spick
Map by Mark Probert
Production managed by Sue Cooper, Bradt & Page Bros

The right of Mark Probert to be identified as the author of this work has been asserted by him in accordance with the Copyright, Designs & Patents Act 1988.

All rights reserved. All views expressed in this book are the views of the author and not those of the publisher. No part of this publication may be reproduced, stored in a retrieval system, or transmitted in any form or by any means, electronic, mechanical, photocopying, recording or otherwise without the prior consent of the publisher.

ISBN: 9781784779863
British Library Cataloguing in Publication Data
A catalogue record for this book is available from the British Library

Photographs
All photographs Mark Probert except the following images from www.shutterstock.com: The Stone Chariot, Hampi (Veerami); The Chinese Fishing Nets, Kochi (Photoestetica); Meenakshi Amman Temple, Madurai (Krishna4079)

Digital conversion by www.dataworks.co.in
Printed in the UK by Page Bros

To find out more about our Journey Books imprint,
visit www.bradtguides.com/journeybooks

Disclaimer
This book depicts events in the author's life as truthfully as recollection permits, which he readily admits, becomes increasingly vague as the years go by. It also depicts events in the life of the author's best friend, Dr Nick Lindsay, and his wife, Mrs Ellen Lindsay, to whom no blame should be attached for anything associated with this publication. This book is not intended to be an academic text; it aims to inform and entertain. Apart from descriptions and opinions provided by the author, this book includes information derived from many sources, including Internet research. ChatGPT has been used in the production of this book, mainly for fact verification, with all the uncertainties that contains. Many more authoritative and academic sources exist; the author's comments on historic events or current affairs provide the briefest of overviews, with the intention of providing context to the events of the journey. The information represented is believed to be correct, but that is only valid if the source and its interpretation are also correct. The publisher apologises for any errors or omissions and would be grateful to be notified of any suggestions for correction to improve the quality of future reprints or editions of this book (please send comments via mgprobert.com). Occasionally, dialogue consistent with the character or nature of the person speaking has been supplemented. Some names, places, and identifying details have been changed to protect the privacy of individuals.

*In memory of that fateful day, in India, in 1947...
when Shirley Vickers met William Probert*

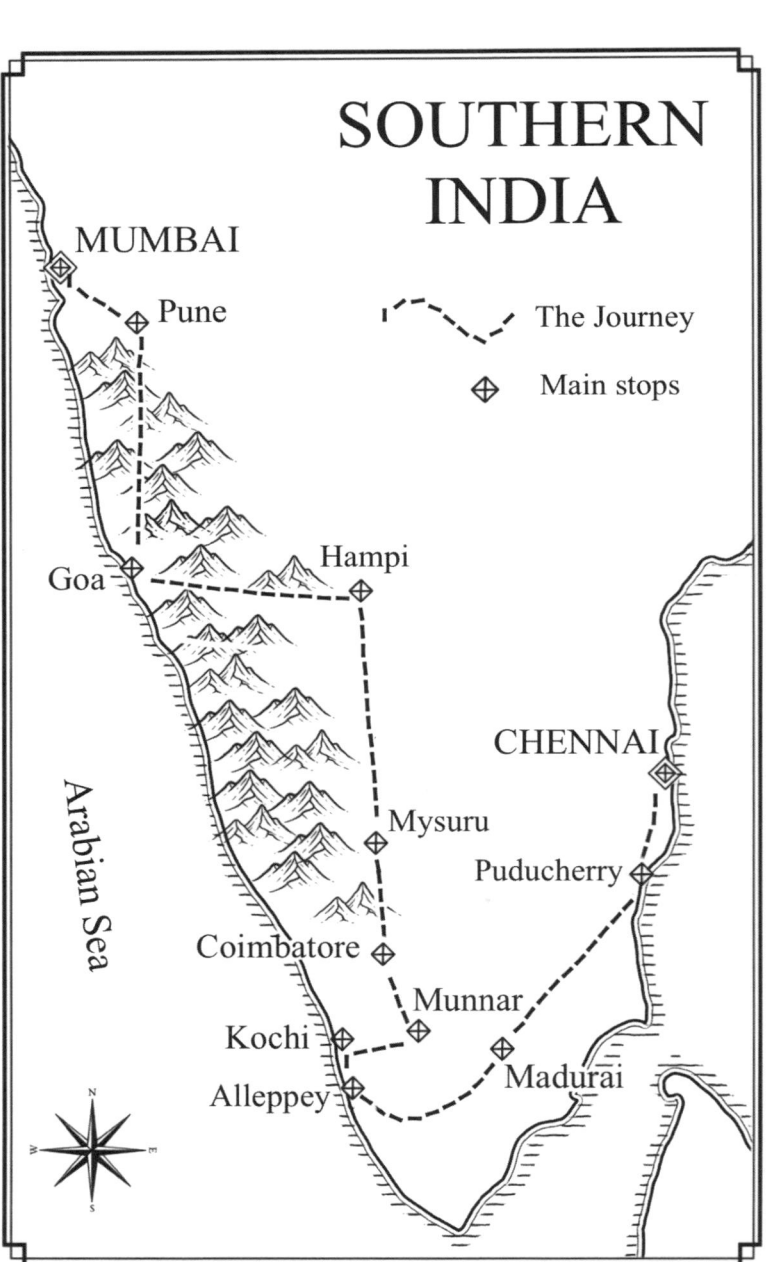

CONTENTS

Before the journey – the background 1

Chapter 1 Bollywood, billionaires, and Bollygarchs 4

Chapter 2 Staying flexible 13

Chapter 3 Schrodinger's airport 30

Chapter 4 Jai Shri Ram! 48

Chapter 5 Mysuru – The day after the night before 73

Chapter 6 The largest bust in the world 90

Chapter 7 It's just your chai talkin' 109

Chapter 8 The Queen of the Arabian Sea 124

Chapter 9 Venice of the East 135

Chapter 10 Goddess Parvati, Jasmine
and a Tyrannosaurus Rex 144

Chapter 11 Fare forward voyagers… but don't be late 154

Chapter 12 'Cooum River, wider than a mile' 179

Reflections 194

Acknowledgements 200

About Mark Probert 202

About Nick Lindsay 203

ILLUSTRATIONS

Indian street politics, Mumbai 11

Aga Khan Palace, Pune 26

Bogmalo Beach, Goa 38

The Stone Chariot, Hampi 55

The Durbar Hall in the Amba Vilas Palace in Mysuru 88

The Adiyogi Shiva, Isha Foundation 96

The hills above Munnar 111

The Chinese Fishing Nets, Kochi 131

Alleppey houseboat 137

Meenakshi Temple, Madurai 146

The Matrimandir, Auroville 168

Chennai Central Station 187

BEFORE THE JOURNEY – THE BACKGROUND

'Jai Shri Ram!' The chant echoed through the ancient streets, a chorus of devotion rising above the clamour of everyday life. I looked at Nick, my intrepid travel companion, and grinned. Here we go again. At sixty something years young, we were about to embark on *another* adventure of a lifetime – a three-week odyssey through the heart of southern India.

India. The name alone conjures up images of vibrant colours, exotic spices, temples, smiling faces, and people hanging out of trains. Until 2020, the country had always been a distant dream for me, for so long a fantastical realm that existed only in the pages of books, the flickering frames of Hindi cinema films and some treasured sepia photos that my Mum and Dad kept in an album. But here we were, two old friends, returning for our second visit together, ready to dive headfirst again into the chaos and beauty of this incredible country.

Our previous visit, almost four years earlier, had taken us across northern India. Over the course of five weeks, Dr Nick Lindsay and I backpacked from Mumbai to Kolkata by train, car, plane, and camel. But this time, things were different. The world had changed since our last visit, and so had we. For three years, the COVID pandemic halted all travel and, more seriously, changed or ended lives forever. It made us all pause, re-evaluate our priorities, and ask ourselves meaningful questions about life and how to live it. And what better place to do that than India, a country that has grappled with the big questions of existence for millennia?

Nick and I have been friends since the mid 1970s. We met on our first day's work at Ordnance Survey, the national mapping agency of Great Britain. He eventually went off to do geological things while I stayed in the world of mapping. Now both retired, we're young-at-heart pensioners who still love to travel.

Before we left India in 2020, we were already thinking about our next trip – there was still so much we wanted to explore, especially in the south of the country. But, as often happens, life — and in this case, a pandemic – got in the way for a while. Our opportunity arose again at the end of 2023.

I was determined that I would leave no stone unturned while preparing for a return to the subcontinent. With southern India as our destination, the potential for chaos was already built in.

First the timing. Trips to India for pale Europeans are best taken in the winter months and that coincided nicely with the 2023 Cricket World Cup. For those who don't know, that's an international tournament of one-day cricket to decide the best team in the world. England were going into the tournament as reigning world champions, and most of the team were vastly experienced in Indian conditions from their participation in the Indian Premier League. England keeping their crown as world number one was a formality. What could go wrong? We'll come back to that one.

My lovely wife Jan gave me the thumbs up for another unsupervised trip abroad. Her logic was faultless, if a little unsettling: 'You don't know how long you've got, so do it while you can.' Although I'm sure it was well intentioned, I thought her comment would be more appropriate for an old person.

Before I got round to planning a route and creating a timetable, I dealt with all the domestic loose ends I could think of… the jobs list, some car maintenance, a boiler service, those outstanding utility bills, etc. The trip would be bookended by World Cup cricket and the annual Chennai 10k race. We just needed to plan the route and work out how to follow it.

We booked tickets for the England v Netherlands World Cup cricket match in Pune at the start of our journey, and registered for the Chennai 10k, due to take place three weeks later. That's a distance of just over 500 miles by plane, but more than 1,000 miles by the meandering route that Nick and I concocted. Our itinerary would include a few recommendations and a selection of touristy 'must-do' sites, selected from a small library of guidebooks and several days researching the internet. It would take us from the bustling streets of Mumbai to the serene backwaters of Kerala, from the ancient temples of Hampi to the experimental township of Auroville. Along that winding route, we would encounter a kaleidoscope of sights, sounds, and experiences that would challenge our assumptions, test our resilience, but ultimately, reaffirm our love for travel and for life itself.

Could the south of India match the big-hitting tourist spots of the north – the magnificence of the Taj Mahal, the raw spiritual energy of Varanasi, the spectacle of the Golden Temple in Amritsar, and the serenity of Bodh Gaya? We were about to find out.

I could think of only one potential spanner that could disrupt my immaculately planned works: Would our pub quiz team be able to compete in one quiz without me? Jan was very reassuring. 'They'll just have to manage somehow,' she said, quietly adding, 'Maybe they won't come last for once.'

Nick booked the flights and I stocked up on the Imodium – we were going to southern India!

CHAPTER 1

BOLLYWOOD, BILLIONAIRES, AND BOLLYGARCHS

Mumbai, formerly known as Bombay, is located on India's western coast, overlooking the Arabian Sea. The city's name was officially changed to Mumbai in 1995 by the government of Maharashtra, the state in which it is situated. 'Mumbai' is derived from 'Mumbā,' the name of the local Hindu goddess Mumbadevi, and 'Aai,' meaning 'mother' in Marathi, the regional language.

As the country's most populous city, with 21 million residents, it also ranks as the sixth largest by population in the world. Serving as the capital of Maharashtra state, Mumbai wears many hats: it is the financial, commercial, and entertainment hub of India. This bustling metropolis is famous for Bollywood, billionaires, and 'Bollygarchs' – a term for those who have amassed significant power, influence, and wealth through their connections in the world of movies. Home to India's world-renowned film industry, Mumbai boasts 92 billionaires, more than any other Asian city. Nick and I are considerably closer to the other end of the wealth and influence spectrum than the Bollygarchs, but for one night, we could call Mumbai our home. It was through this gateway to India that we entered on 5th November 2023, to mark the beginning of our three-week adventure through the southern states of the country.

Our Mumbai journey kicked off at 11:00 am local time, although our internal clocks were still stubbornly clinging to the early hours of back home. We hadn't planned to stay long in Mumbai, and we didn't. The brevity of our stopover felt somewhat disrespectful to the city, yet it mirrored the perennial traveller's dilemma – whether to linger awhile and fully immerse in a place or to venture forth in pursuit of fresh destinations and experiences. I've still not worked out which approach is best, but I usually tend towards the latter.

We were beginning our trip as we planned to continue – with indecent haste. A single night to recover from our ten-hour flight from London and we would, in theory, be good to go again. We had an early-morning flight to Pune booked for the next day.

A long-haul flight is never a pleasant experience, but the discomfort is soon forgotten with the excitement of landing somewhere exotic. Even though I'm now technically in my seventies, on a purely numerical basis, I still get very excited when I arrive in an unfamiliar land, far from home. Having some sort of arrival strategy is always a good idea, especially if, like me, you exist in a semi-zombie state for several hours after landing. Our plan was simple – collect our baggage, find an ATM, get a taxi to our hotel, check in, find a local SIM card… then catch up on some sleep.

When we arrived on our previous visit to the city four years earlier, the airport seemed strangely quiet. It was the same this time. We found the taxi firm that employs only female drivers, as on our last visit, and we were again driven to our hotel with minimal fuss and, for the most part, on the correct side of the road. Once out of the air-conditioned micro-climates of the airport and the taxi, we were enveloped in lovely 30-degree warmth – the dull winter greyness of London melting away like yesterday's worries.

As if stepping out of the opening scenes of the movie *The Wizard of Oz*, Nick and I had arrived from a faraway land of black and white. As we ventured onto the streets of Mumbai, the scene shifted to vibrant colour to signify our arrival in the fantastical world that is India. Despite having experienced a sensory assault from this outrageous Bombay mix once before, it still hit me like a Diwali firecracker, scattering a thousand brilliant shards of raw sensation... a shock and awe rude awakening for a pensioner who was still only twenty-four hours away from rural Dorset.

In just half an hour, we were transported from the serene library vibes of the airport arrivals hall to the commotion of suburban Mumbai. Amid a swirling haze of fumes and pollution, traffic raced at breakneck speed. Tuk-tuks buzzed like furious wasps, overloaded motorcycles roared like thundering beasts, and dilapidated buses coughed up clouds of black diesel smoke as if on their last breath. It was a lively symphony of engines, voices, screeching brakes, and incessant honking. And the symphony was being played at high volume.

We were driven past hundreds of overstocked little shops bursting onto the pavements with everything imaginable, but especially, it seemed, kitchen utensils, bananas, scraggy chickens, colourful saris, mobile phones, and granite work surfaces. The scene unfolded in a colourful kaleidoscope of tumbling shapes, as thousands of people rushed to places that others had just vacated. And then there's the smell, oh, the smell.

Our hotel was in Vakola, an igneous intrusion of a suburb that appeared to be dominated by one product. They may not be the most practical gifts for a tourist to take home, but if it's a new kitchen work surface you're looking for, you could do worse than a visit to Vakola. Slabs of shiny granite seemed to be everywhere.

Not even the most tongue-in-cheek estate agents' blurb would have the nerve to describe the area as attractive, but our hotel's location, just over a mile from the airport, made it handy for our brief overnight stopover. This positive attribute was something I felt I needed to strongly emphasise to Nick when we finally caught sight of our overnight accommodation. We found our dreary-looking hotel hiding apologetically among a sea of colourful shopfronts. Most were adorned with adverts and flickering neon signs that whispered promises of hidden treasures within. Those hidden treasures were mainly in the form of stone-based consumer products – worktops, floor tiles, wall tiles, and memorial stones. We had unwittingly stumbled upon the stone and granite retail hub of Mumbai. Every other shop was selling worktops, windows aglow with bright lights that cast a sparkly luminescence upon countless rows of polished slabs. A short distance further down the road from our hotel, a noisy political rally was in full swing, a sea of white-and-orange-clothed and highly charged activists. The already noisy street was being pumped even louder with the impassioned cries of fervent party supporters.

Drab functional would be a generous description of our hotel. Our previous experience in India had led us to expect better. On the positive side, once into our small room, the mattresses were firm, and the en-suite shower room was almost spotless. In order to keep my eyes open and avoid slurring my words, I needed a brief nap. I checked my fitness-tracker watch to see if my body battery was indicating any signs of life. It was reading 5 per cent, and when I awoke a couple of hours later, it was still 5 per cent. It doesn't show anything lower. I was flatlining, but Nick said he was bursting with energy, so we reassessed the arrival plan and wandered into the chaos of the street to find some local SIM cards for our phones.

The young lad in the ramshackle phone shop we found a few doors away told us his dad would need to be present to provide us with 'passport SIM cards'. Unfortunately, his dad was somewhere else… but no problem, he would be back 'some time'. Our helpful assistant said 'also Vodafone shop is just down the road'.

The former Vodafone shop he was referring to had been stripped bare, leaving a man sitting in silent vigil on a single white plastic chair in the middle of the space, as if on guard duty. 'You go two doors down,' the man in the chair said, suddenly recalling his role as second clue in our treasure hunt, 'just beyond the granite shop'. After walking about 200 metres in the direction he'd pointed, all we found were more granite shops and a tiny butcher's shop stacked high with cages of tightly packed, highly distressed chickens. The chicken vendor clearly hadn't read the memo about having to sell granite-based products. We stopped briefly to watch a toothless artisan chiselling names into a memorial stone on the dusty pavement. He worked swiftly, and with meticulous care, despite the attention of two lairy old foreign chaps taking photos and asking silly questions.

Each time I set off on one of my travel adventures like this I wonder if the usual quota of crazy incidents will keep happening. In India, it's a reasonable bet that you will come across unusual things. On the first day of our last visit to Mumbai, Nick and I had narrowly avoided arrest. What could possibly happen this time?

Our search for SIM cards came to an abrupt halt when we encountered the political rally that we'd heard earlier making all the noise. A stage had been set up at the side of the road upon which, sat cross-legged, were a group of activists in white robes, with bright orange scarves and hats. Their message, whatever it was, boomed out in the local Marathi language from huge speakers, and was met with a deafening chorus of toots and honks from passing vehicles as drivers slowed down to show their approval. A crowd of maybe a hundred people milled around the stage, and began chanting whenever prompted. As we attempted to shuffle our way through, avoiding stepping into the traffic, a young chap dressed in an immaculate white and orange outfit came over to us, asked us for a couple of selfies, and then invited us onto the stage.

Small political rallies like this are relatively common in India, but it's not something we're familiar with in Britain. At this rally, the socialist party from Maharashtra was advocating for greater rights for the lowest members of the caste system. Our unexpected encounter with the gathering offered insight into a topical and controversial political issue in India.

The caste system has played a pivotal role in shaping India's narrative for centuries. It's a Hindu thing, and as approximately 80 per cent of the Indian population are Hindu, the caste system affects all aspects of society. Rooted in scriptures thousands of years old, the caste system carefully divides individuals into distinct hierarchical groups, each with specific roles and expectations. At its core are the four primary castes 'Brahmins, Kshatriyas, Vaishyas, and Shudras' each believed to have emerged from the hands of Brahma, the Hindu god of creation. These four categories, each with its designated purpose in society, have formed the bedrock of the caste system. The structure extends far beyond those four, however, branching into a labyrinth of around 3,000 castes and 25,000 sub-castes, each assigned specific occupations within carefully defined layers of society. Beyond this complex framework lay the unfortunate Achhoots or Dalits – 'the untouchables'. Readers of *Journey through India* may recall the description of the Doms of Varanasi – the Dalits with the specific job of 'keepers of the fires' on the banks of the holy Ganges.

The caste system perpetuates social inequality and discrimination, denying Dalits equal access to education, employment, and housing. Despite the constitutional efforts to eradicate caste-based discrimination in the post-1947 independence period, the system's deep roots persist, permeating all aspects of life, from personal relationships to educational opportunities, access to resources, and of course, politics.

The results of a population census in Bihar, a rural state in the east of India, in October 2023, created political shockwaves that reverberated at the national level. The first caste census since independence revealed that over two-thirds of the state's population belonged to communities classified as 'backward or marginalised'. These findings not only reignited the debate on societal injustices in India, but also spurred calls for new policies to ensure fair opportunities for all citizens. Despite India being the world's fifth-largest economy, a significant wealth gap persists between its richest and poorest classes. This stark inequality, highlighted by the Bihar census results, prompted previously marginalised groups to demand social justice and political representation.

Because of the Bihar census, the caste system – with all its complexities and enduring influence – had become the subject of heated national political debate just at the time that Nick and I arrived in Mumbai. It was the big topic the local socialist party was fervently promoting during their rally. Like the innocent foreigners abroad that we were, we marched onto the stage and

Indian street politics, Mumbai

donned our orange hats and scarves. Taking the microphone and naively repeating the party's rallying cries in the local Marathi language we could have been saying anything. We were inciting an armed uprising against the government for all we knew, but our pronouncements were met with delirious cheers and growing excitement from the crowd in front of the stage.

I can't say it was a typical Monday afternoon for me; I'd normally have a ninety-minute yoga class and then go home for an afternoon nap.

A group of heavily armed police officers slumped lazily in flimsy white plastic chairs at one side of the stage. Perhaps they'd borrowed them from the man in the Vodafone shop. They looked totally disinterested, with most of them turning to their phones for entertainment. We took this as a good sign – interpreting their inaction as reassurance that we weren't about to be arrested. By now, Nick was enjoying himself with the microphone far too much – I'm not sure what he was saying, something about brotherly support, but he was arousing the crowd to ever greater heights. It reminded me of his appearance on national TV during our last visit to India. Give him a microphone and the limelight for a moment and he transforms into a showman driven by an insatiable need to mesmerise an audience. And I must admit, he's bloody good at it. I managed to pry him away from the stage before he got as far as signing the forms to stand for the national elections, and we went in search of the vegetarian restaurant our young activist friend had recommended to us. 'Just mention my name… and the party – they will give you very good meal.'

It felt like our adventure was truly underway – after just five hours in India, we'd already managed to stir up local political unrest and nearly brought the Mumbai traffic to a standstill. We set off in search of the veggie restaurant. Not a bad start, and as it turned out, we had an excellent curry. The SIM cards had to wait.

CHAPTER 2

STAYING FLEXIBLE

On our first full day back in India, with our body clocks still struggling to reset, Nick and I were up early for the short taxi ride back to Mumbai airport. I can't recall why we thought it was a good idea to take a flight to go just 75 miles to Pune (pronounced Poonay) but it must have made sense at the time we booked it.

Pune is a vibrant city of over 3 million people, situated on the Deccan plateau southeast of Mumbai. During my research for the visit, I discovered that in recent years the city had secured the top spot in the Indian Government's 'Ease of Living' Index. The city's renowned educational system, vibrant culture, growing economy, and pleasant weather all contributed to its high score. In addition, Pune scores highly in infrastructure, public services, sanitation, and greenery. The pleasant weather and greenery came out to meet us as we took our taxi ride from the airport to the hotel. While high sanitation scores are always welcome at any travel destination, Nick and I were mainly visiting Pune for cricket and yoga – though not both at the same time.

The timing of our trip to southern India had been dictated by the 2023 Cricket World Cup. Nick and I wanted to watch at least one game, and maybe more if England got through to the latter stages of the tournament. As reigning world champions in the one-day format, success was a given. I made the mistake of not informing the England and Wales Cricket Board of our plans, however, and by the time we got to see the England team in action they had already been eliminated from the knockout stages of the competition. We'd bought the tickets though, and a cricket match in India is always an occasion, so we flew to Pune looking forward to watching the England v Netherlands group-stage match.

The other main reason to visit Pune was to visit the world-famous Ramamani Iyengar Memorial Yoga Institute (RIMYI). When I began attending regular yoga classes in 2021, I chose to follow the Iyengar style. Named after B.K.S. Iyengar, this form of yoga was developed by a man who overcame physical limitations and poor health to become a global yoga icon. Affectionately known as Guruji, he captivated students with his wisdom, rigorous approach, and humour. He is credited with helping to introduce yoga to the West, and his bestselling books, like *Light on Yoga*, have demystified the practice for millions. Although he passed away in 2014, the institute he founded continues to thrive under the guidance of his son, Prashant Iyengar. Before I flew to India, my yoga teacher helped arrange a meeting with Prashant Iyengar.

I breathed a sigh of relief when our taxi from Pune airport brought us to the Shantai Hotel, near to the city centre. It was like a breath of fresh air after our previous night's accommodation – clean, tidy, and surrounded by Pune's famous greenery. With two excellent restaurants on-site, it was the perfect place to settle in for three nights.

We'd been in India for twenty-four hours and hadn't visited a single temple, so as soon as we checked in, Nick and I headed for the Dagadusheth Halwai Ganapati Temple, just a thirty-minute walk from our hotel. Temples are a key part of life in India and we felt an early visit would make us feel we were really back. That short walk gave us a taste of the mixed flavours of Pune. Passing by the tall ramparts of Shaniwar Wada Palace, the great seat of the Peshwas of the Maratha Empire, we could feel the weight of history. It was the centre of power in the Indian subcontinent for the larger part of the eighteenth century. We were walking where the Rashtrakutas built empires, the Mughals left their mark in opulent gardens, and the famous Maratha cavalry thundered through the surrounding valleys. Rich in history, Pune is also adapting to the demands of the modern world and those new rhythms dance side by side with the echoes of the past. Ancient empires have left their mark, while sleek, modern buildings rise among bustling bazaars. In sun-drenched squares, tradition sips chai from clay cups, while innovation brews in sleek cafes fuelled by caffeine and ambition. Pune, known as the 'Oxford of the East,' is a curious mixture of old and new – a city where centuries-old banyan trees shade students poring over textbooks, and young entrepreneurs dream of disrupting the digital world, one algorithm at a time.

By mid-morning, we arrived, hot and sticky, at the Dagadusheth Halwai Ganapati Temple, near the heart of the city. Built in 1893 from white marble, it nestles amid fragrant spice shops and vibrant market stalls in a typically crowded and bustling part of central Pune. In Hinduism, temple worship allows devotees to connect with the divine in a sacred, tangible space. Temples are considered the earthly abodes of gods and goddesses, where worshippers offer prayers, perform rituals, and seek blessings. A key element of Hindu temple worship is darshan – the act of seeing and being seen by the deity. Hindus believe that the divine presence is embodied in the temple's images or symbols – such as statues of deities, like Ganesha in the Dagadusheth Halwai

Ganapati Temple. This reflects the belief that God can manifest in many forms. Viewing these sacred representations is thought to bestow spiritual benefits, as it enables devotees to receive the deity's grace and favour, making a tangible connection to the divine in this life, not just the next.

I should explain that temple name: first, Ganapati. This is one of 108 alternative names used in the Hindu scriptures for Ganesha, the very popular pot-bellied deity with four arms and the head of an elephant. There are, depending on your sources, up to 330 million deities in Hindu scriptures. Although the number is vast, many of them are personifications of concepts, aspects of other deities, or regional interpretations.

Hindus often focus on a prominent trinity: Brahma (the Creator), Vishnu (the Preserver), and Shiva (the Destroyer). These represent different aspects of the supreme Brahman, and this universal one, the one ultimate reality, underlies all deities and creation. Ganesha or Ganapati is the son of Shiva and Parvati and is known as the god of new beginnings and remover of obstacles. We all need one of those in our lives. Nick and I became very fond of him on our previous visit to India, so it seemed only right to pay our respects at the new beginning of our latest trip, just in case we encountered any obstacles that needed removing. We were two of the 100,000-plus visitors each year who visit what is described in some sources as the second most popular temple dedicated to Ganesha in India.

Temples also play a vital role in the community, serving as centres for cultural, educational, and social activities. They are gathering places for festivals, rituals, and community events, reinforcing social bonds and shared cultural values. This communal aspect of temple worship fosters a sense of belonging and helps preserve traditions across generations.

We left our footwear with the official shoe minder and walked barefoot across the street to join a large crowd of people heading for the temple entrance. Waved inside with beaming smiles and friendly wobbles of the head by the uniformed men minding the security scanners, we stepped through the intricately carved gates of the temple and followed the line of pilgrims that snaked around the inside of the building.

The Dagadusheth Halwai Ganapati Temple is unusual in being named after a devotee rather than a deity. Its eponymous founder, Dagadusheth Halwai, was a sweet maker who lived in Pune over 150 years ago. In the late 19th century, he was devastated by the loss of his only son to an epidemic that swept through the city. His guru, Madhavnath Maharaj, suggested that Dagadusheth and his wife could build a Ganapati temple to help heal their grief and bring hope amid their suffering. They followed his advice, and in addition to building the temple, the couple began addressing social issues in the community – a tradition that continues today. The temple is not only a place of worship but also a centre for social initiatives, offering micro-finance for small businesses and a care home for senior citizens. The temple's support for deprived children struck a chord with Nick, especially as it had been less than twenty-four hours since he'd stood on stage wearing an orange hat, microphone in hand, thrust into the role of political spokesperson for the socially disadvantaged people of Maharashtra.

Sensory overload is an expression that's often overused when describing India, but as Nick and I entered the temple, everything seemed to go up another level, bursting into a synthesised medley of stimuli. Sunlight made distorted stained-glass mosaics dance across the floor and the air vibrated with the sound of chanting and the gentle, rhythmic ringing of hand bells. The marble floor, polished by decades of pilgrims' bare footsteps, echoed the countless prayers offered over the years. Some visitors stood, others sat meditating, some were on their own and others were in small groups, quietly humming their devotion to Ganesha in a gentle chorus. Everywhere we looked, there were offerings – piles of coconuts, baskets of colourful fruits and flowers, and ghee lamps flickering like a constellation of tiny stars. Faith hung heavy in the air, etched into the faces of devotees, many of whom were dressed in simple white or orange robes. This place is hugely important to them. Their faces showed that most of them were somewhere else entirely. And at the heart of it all, watching benignly over proceedings, sits a large Ganesha – just over 2 metres tall and covered with 40 kilos of gold. Adorned with a constantly refreshed stream of offerings, his gentle eyes provide a comforting welcome to all who seek sanctuary and spiritual support. For most visitors, a visit to the temple holds immense significance – and you need to understand just how significant religion is in India to understand the country itself.

Hinduism permeates all parts of the cultural landscape, shaping India's social structures, traditions, festivals, and daily routines. Hinduism, Buddhism, Jainism, and Sikhism all originated in India, contributing to the nation's diverse cultural and social fabric. They complement and contrast each other in a complex pattern, interwoven with the twin strands of Islam and Christianity. Sometimes, tensions fray the edges of this intricate weave, with religious identity occasionally fuelling social and political conflicts. Yet, within the sanctuary of the Dagadusheth

Halwai Ganpati Temple, religion seems to transcend any tensions simmering outside, binding families, friends, and communities together. Here, for a short while at least, worshippers can find the solace, purpose, and a sense of belonging that they, and most of us, seek.

Rows of Ganesha models of all shapes, sizes, and colours filled the shelves of the souvenir shop on the way out of the temple. They seemed to curl their trunks towards the lines of people shuffling slowly past, pleading to be taken home. A bright pink one, made of plaster and about 3 inches high shouted out to me to take him with me. Even at a modest 3 inches tall, he looked majestic – his proportions seemed purposely designed for an elderly English chap to carry around India for three weeks. I liked him so much I bought two.

One of the expected highlights of our three-week adventure was in the diary for midday, and I didn't want to miss it. Nick negotiated us a favourable tuk-tuk deal and half an hour later we were stood outside the famous RIMYI Iyengar yoga centre, on the west side of the city. After making ourselves known to the people at the reception desk, we removed our shoes and waited patiently, watching a stream of people walk in and out of the main exercise studio. There was a very diverse range of shapes, sizes, colours, and ages, but the slim, fit, and flexible female category was in the majority. Before I go any further, I should write a few brief words about what yoga is, for those who might not be familiar with the subject. I apologise to those who are.

To many people yoga looks like a series of physical postures performed with varying degrees of ease or discomfort by people in trendy gym-wear on plastic mats. That's how it seemed to me until 3 years ago, and if that's what you want it to be, it can be that. I soon discovered, however, yoga has many aspects, encompassing physical, mental, and spiritual disciplines. Yoga's history stretches back thousands of years and is rooted in Hindu and Buddhist traditions – but it is not a religion. Ancient texts like the *Yoga Sutras* by Patanjali (depending on sources, this dates from anywhere between 322BC to the 5th century CE) describe eight limbs, or aspects to yoga, including ethical principles, postures, breath control, meditation, and more. These practices were followed in ancient times in order to find and enter a state of deep peace, heightened awareness, and even harmony with the divine. For the time being, let's call yoga a philosophy that offers pathways to self-discovery and well-being. Over time, various classical branches have emerged, like Hatha yoga and Raja yoga, emphasising different aspects of those original eight limbs. Modern yoga includes newer styles such as the flowing Vinyasa styles, the orderly Ashtanga yoga or Iyengar yoga that focuses on precise alignment and use of props.

When I began attending yoga classes, my initial aim was to maintain some physical fitness and to keep or improve a range of movement that would otherwise decline with age. I've found those benefits, but yoga has also opened a door into something else. Physically, I can vouch for it promoting flexibility, strength, and balance. It improves posture and reduces pain, although it can sometimes be exhausting and my knees still click. Mentally, I feel that it helps to reduce stress and anxiety, while improving focus. That dull physical ache I feel after lessons proves I've been trying, and mentally I always feel so much better leaving the class than when I arrived. The most intriguing yet elusive benefit, often talked about in yoga, is the potential for self-awareness, inner peace, and a sense of connection to something larger. That's interesting, isn't it? Countless practitioners, regardless of background, report these benefits, suggesting it's more than just wishful thinking. That brings us back to Pune and waiting in the RIMYI yoga centre for Prashant Iyengar.

Prashant arrived precisely at midday, immediately putting Nick and me at ease. He suggested a more private spot for our meeting. He found us chairs, and then sat cross-legged on a bed, radiating calm. I thought, 'This is what someone who has got it all together looks like.' We worked through my questions methodically, yet the conversation felt like a relaxed chat. Prashant's long and thoughtful answers made it a bit one-sided, but he was generous with his time and comfortable with me recording the discussion. Prashant Iyengar is a deep thinker who believes it was his destiny to devote his life to yoga. He sees it as a comprehensive path that covers every aspect of human development. When I asked if he found the Western view of yoga as mere 'exercise' frustrating, he responded with patient understanding. He acknowledged that this view isn't limited to the West and believes that even if people start yoga for physical benefits, teachers can gradually introduce them to its deeper aspects. Yoga, he explained, doesn't eliminate life's problems but helps people cope with them. This approach also applies to how he and his father taught asanas (physical exercises) while gradually introducing other limbs of yoga. I was particularly interested in samadhi, considered by some the ultimate aim of yoga – a state of transcendental awareness beyond ordinary perceptions. When I asked if Prashant had experienced samadhi, he explained that striving for it as a goal contradicts yoga's principle of dispassion. He shared an Indian saint's wisdom: 'If you say yes, you have not achieved it.' Prashant added, 'We cannot say what the ultimate end of yoga is… we are only in pursuit of it.' When I asked for a single takeaway from our discussion, Prashant's response was profound: 'After being born as a human being, we have to become human beings. Yoga is something that makes you a human being.' This conversation, which I hope I've captured faithfully, offered great wisdom and shifted our three-week trip onto a more spiritual course. Unhurried, Prashant signed a copy of his book for me with a warm smile, and then returned to his teaching duties.

Brimming with gratitude, but stomachs grumbling with hunger, Nick and I sought refuge in the nearby Shabree restaurant, eager to debrief over a plate of their famed thali. As fate would have it, our table was positioned beside a lively group of eight Pune ladies of a certain age. They were having a great time. We worked out they were old school friends who met regularly over good food and even better gossip. On this occasion, the whispers revolved around us, but after the obligatory selfie flurry, we soon found ourselves absorbed into their circle, engulfed by the energy of the group and endless anecdotes they were eager to tell us. The ladies were charming and utterly captivating. One regaled us with tales of Pune's bygone era, immersing us in the sepia-toned richness of its post-colonial past. Another described her visits with her husband to Britain over the years, while a third graciously shared her sage advice on mastering the alchemy of brewing the perfect cup of chai. After warm farewells, two well-fed Brits stumbled back into the chaos of Pune, invigorated by the hospitality and charm of eight extraordinary ladies.

I'd hogged the agenda for the day with our visit to the RIMYI yoga centre, so the last visit of the day was mainly for Nick. Back home on his highland estate he is chairperson of the Clyne Heritage Society, and he is never happier than when he's looking at old things, as long as it's not me. We headed for the Raja Dinkar Kelkar Museum, a distinctive building almost hidden amid the narrow lanes of Pune's old town. This museum houses the one-man collection of the late Dr D.G. Kelkar (1896–1990), who spent decades amassing an impressive private collection of over 20,000 objects showcasing India's rich cultural heritage. The artefacts range widely, from textiles and kitchenware to musical instruments and weapons. Dr Kelkar established the museum in 1962 and later donated it to the government in 1975.

Strange things happen when you go to India. I'm not sure what it is, but I don't think similar things happen to me in 'normal' life. And here was another example. Nick got into a conversation with a member of staff who told him the museum was trying to secure funding for larger premises. Limited space and funding meant that only 2,500 items of the museum's collection can be displayed, leaving 85 per cent of it unseen and vulnerable to deterioration. Back home in the Highlands Nick was wrestling with similar relocation issues with his local heritage centre. I thought I'd just left them talking about 'old things' but somehow it all escalated while I wasn't watching.

The next thing I knew, we were sitting in the museum director's office, drinking tea and talking about funding. After an extensive tour of the museum, the director, Sudhanva Hari Ranade, now great friends with Nick, took us into the private section — the part that extends into his own residence. Before I knew it, we were seated on an ornate sofa, as if on a Bollywood film set, surrounded by beautifully decorated doorways and carved pillars from the relocated Mastani Mahal Palace, originally built in 1734.

As if that wasn't enough, we were then whisked outside for selfies next to the director's private Ganesha temple. I should mention that Ganesha is the patron deity of Maharashtra, so for Ganesha enthusiasts like Nick and me, the sight of yet another temple dedicated to our favourite deity shouldn't really have come as a surprise.

After a while in India, nothing comes as a surprise. Sudhanva shared his ambitious plans for the collection, detailing his 'Museum City' project, which aims to develop a world-class museum complex with state-of-the-art display techniques, research facilities, and an institute of museology (I had no idea such things existed). I hope that by the time this book is published, at least two relocation projects will be underway — one in India and one in Scotland.

We ended our meeting with an exchange of contact details and warm promises to keep in touch before the three of us went our separate ways. Not for the first time in India, Nick and I had experienced wonderful hospitality, and over dinner that evening, we reflected on a typical day filled with diverse experiences. From Ganesha to yogic enlightenment, the Pune ladies' social club, a Maratha palace, and back to Ganesha again.

STAYING FLEXIBLE

Day two of our visit to Pune was reserved for cricket, but because it was a day/night match we still had a good chunk of the day available for sightseeing. One sight we really needed to see was the ticket office. I had a receipt from purchasing the tickets online but we needed to collect the physical versions before the game. Non-cricket fans – don't panic, I'll keep this very brief. If you are keen, however, please see *Journey through India*, in which there is an entire chapter dedicated to a one-day international match between India and Australia.

Ganesha was smiling on us. I had assumed, I think reasonably, that the ticket office would be at the Maharashtra Cricket Association (MCA) Stadium, where the game was due to be played. Our plans for the day had to include travelling 15 miles out of town to get to the stadium in plenty of time to collect the tickets before the match. By chance (or cleverly arranged by Ganesha) Nick and I bumped into two other cricket fans next to the toaster in our hotel at breakfast time. In our discussions over lift sharing they told us the tickets couldn't be collected at the ground. We needed to go just a short distance down the road from the hotel, in central Pune, to pick them up. That might have been very annoying later in the day if we hadn't found out.

After collecting the tickets – a surprisingly straightforward process – we found ourselves with a palace-sized gap in the rest of the day. I don't normally remember individual tuk-tuk rides, but the one to the Aga Khan Palace, driven by a man who was part Virat Kohli, part Mad Max, was unforgettable. Heading northeast, our driver decided it would be a bit of a wheeze if he took us up the wrong side of a dual carriageway. The journey had been relatively uneventful until then, and we were nearly at our destination. A few yards on a quiet road is one thing, but this was a couple of hundred metres into speeding traffic, with lorries, cars, and motorcycles coming past us at 50 miles per hour-plus from the opposite direction. Somehow, Mad Max managed to pull off this high-tariff manoeuvre without involving the emergency services, elevating his status among other Pune taxi drivers and saving us about half a mile. We arrived unscathed, so that's fair enough.

Pune's Aga Khan Palace was built in 1892 by Sultan Mohammed Shah Aga Khan III, the spiritual leader of the Nizari Ismaili Muslims. When a devastating famine struck the region, the Aga Khan provided work to over 1,000 affected villagers by employing them

Aga Khan Palace, Pune

to construct the palace. It's a majestic building that blends graceful Italian arches with intricate Indian carvings. Its story, however, took a poignant turn in 1942 when it became Mahatma Gandhi's prison during the Quit India Movement. His wife Kasturba and secretary Mahadev Desai shared his confinement (they both died there), within the palace walls, which must have witnessed long and fascinating debates about India's future. The palace now stands as a national memorial, its serene beauty forever linked with that pivotal chapter in Gandhi's life and India's fight for freedom. We wandered around the rooms and read the history of the place from the information boards. One of the most poignant exhibits displays Gandhi's simple bed and his worn sandals. They look so silent and modest in contrast to the grandeur of the building, but that contrast somehow emphasises his resilience and strength.

The grounds were a quiet green haven surrounded by the crazy bustle of Pune. As we wandered around, we came across Gandhi's 'samadhi'. It's a modest memorial that holds some of Gandhi's ashes. The Aga Khan Palace is a place of pilgrimage for millions seeking inspiration from a visionary leader who played a pivotal role in shaping the political landscape of India. I need to explain a little more, because later on our trip we came across the great man's ashes once again in the Gandhi Memorial Museum in Madurai. In 1948, the majority of Gandhi's ashes were ceremonially immersed at the Triveni Sangam in Allahabad, where the mythical Ganges, Yamuna, and Saraswati rivers converge. That location holds immense religious significance for Hindus and symbolises the return of a soul to the universal Brahman. However, his family kept a small portion of the ashes and dispersed them at several other locations, including the Aga Khan Palace in Pune.

After soaking up the grandeur of the Aga Khan Palace, we were ready to transition from the historical importance of the past to the light-hearted excitement of a cricket match at the Pune MCA stadium – that's quite a contrast. It took almost an hour to get out of the city to the stadium; long enough for us to transition from history buffs to Barmy Army. Being in India, we weren't too surprised when the taxi driver dumped us on a dirt track on a patch of rough ground well over a mile from the cricket stadium. He shrugged his shoulders as if to say 'job done, not my problem' as he told us that any further was a no-entry zone for taxis.

We trudged our way slowly to the ground in the heat of the afternoon. Surprisingly, or maybe not given England's dire form, there was hardly anyone else around with only about two hours to go before the game started. Being in India, we weren't surprised either when a couple of ex-professional Indian cricketers very kindly stopped their car on their way to their VIP box and gave us a lift to the doors of the stadium. Thank you again, Indrajeet Kamtekar and Parag Shahane, you are true gentlemen and our new sporting heroes.

Let's not dwell long on the match – it was a magnificent stadium, a sparse crowd, and in the context of the tournament, a meaningless game. At the end of the England innings a few red kites soared in lazy circles high above the pitch to inject a bit of ornithological interest. Occasional gusts of wind dispersed the heat of the late afternoon sun and pushed some dark grey storm clouds around and past the stadium. The weather forecast gave us a 50-50 chance of rain, but in the event we were lucky – we just had a few drops, and they fell during the change of innings. The scene provided a perfect metaphor for England's disastrous tournament and gave Nick and me the chance to indulge in some amateur sports reporting… 'England's hopes ebbed faster than the fading light and birds of prey circled over the sorry remains of their World Cup challenge, while storm clouds of supporter discontent gathered menacingly in the background.' Well, it kept us amused.

The day's entertainment was saved by the excitement and artistry of a Ben Stokes' rapid-fire century, and a rare England victory. We just had to get back to the hotel after that – which involved several hours, several cancelled Uber rides, and lots of walking in the dark.

Throughout our time in Pune, Nick and I kept seeing large painted signs along the side of the road for the recent G20 meetings in India. Its twelve months presidency of the G20 had only just ended, concluding with the New Delhi summit in September 2023. During that year, numerous G20 meetings took place across India with an overarching theme of 'Vasudhaiva Kutumbakam' or 'One Earth · One Family · One Future,' emphasising the need for global cooperation and unity in addressing shared challenges. It's a reminder of just how much India has become a major global player on the world stage. The world's most populous country is also its fifth-largest economy, and it has sent missions to the moon and Mars. Our next mission was to get to Goa, and our flight was early the next morning.

CHAPTER 3

SCHRODINGER'S AIRPORT

The only good thing about picking the craziest tuk-tuk driver in Pune to take us to the Aga Khan Palace was that, statistically, with up to 10,000 alternatives to choose from, we would be very unfortunate to have the same guy again the following day when we had to go to the airport for our flight to Goa. Instead, we must have picked his twin brother.

I touched upon Indian driving in my book *Journey through India*. For those who haven't read it, I'll briefly summarise how the Indian version of driving differs from what you might be used to in countries with a more rule-based approach. In principle, they drive on the left in India – it should be simple, right?

Back in the calm embrace of the British road network, we bask in the luxury of predictability, with laws like the Highways Act 1980 and the Road Traffic Act 1988 creating a structured and dependable environment. The Highway Code supplements this legal framework, promoting safety and efficiency for those who venture out onto the nation's roads. Safe stopping distances, roundabout procedures, and a comprehensive range of standardised road signs make our roads a haven of monotonous consistency.

That's how it's meant to be, and, by and large, everyone goes along with the game and stays within the prescribed parameters. It's a cosy world where one can assume that others will stick to their designated side of the road, vehicles are annually scrutinised for roadworthiness, and mandatory insurance cushions the blow of unfortunate mishaps. Now, let's shift our gaze to the whirlwind that is Indian driving.

Picture a two-lane road, akin to a British 'A' or 'B' road, with a sliver of dirt masquerading as a pavement on either side. In India, this modest space, usually made up of tarmac, earth, and potholes, can magically accommodate up to six lanes of traffic. Any combination of traffic direction, on either side of a centre line, is possible. But then who needs a centre line, or indeed any road markings and signs? Mere decorations, akin to a forgotten spice in the back of a cupboard. Brace yourself for wrong-way jaunts on dual carriageways (like yesterday's shortcut) and the occasional cart and horse taking residence in the overtaking lane.

Although Nick and I saw a few women drivers (they were mostly on scooters), the vast majority of drivers are men. The Indian driver sets forth on a journey with an urgent need to 'catch up'. Joining the traffic flow is the first step. No need to look; existing drivers will obviously adjust their course to accommodate the newcomer, accompanied by a harmonious chorus of welcoming car horns.

Overtaking in India is an art, a flamboyant display akin to a peacock flaunting its feathers. It becomes a matter of pride. Failure to get in front of every vehicle ahead is a blow to masculine esteem. Hanging on the tail of the vehicle in front, a high-speed ballet unfolds, culminating in a strategic toot of the car horn and a gradual glide past – it can be either side. The technique of changing down a gear immediately prior to the manoeuvre is, alas, considered unnecessary by the Indian driver, and blind bends are navigated with the optimism of a gambler placing a high-stakes bet… and always relying on others to give way.

Those high-roller odds lengthen as dusk descends and overtaking into the murky unknown becomes an even chancier gamble with the shadows. Forays into the oncoming lane become a series of blind leaps of faith that gradually blur the boundaries between reality and the surreal dance of luck. The potential for an abrupt meeting with something solid and unlit looms large – a final rendezvous, perhaps, with a vehicle for which lights were considered an optional, but surely unnecessary, extra. The bullock pulling its late-evening load of sugarcane back to the village will be blissfully unaware of the need to be seen.

When I first visited the country in 2020, I couldn't understand why so many of the advertising hoardings, billboards, and TV adverts were trying to sell cement. It all makes sense when you realise that the entire country is one enormous construction site, and like much in India, the road network is mostly a work in progress. In many areas you feel you're driving out of one set of road works only to head immediately back into another one. We heard a rumour about a major national road infrastructure project underway across the whole of the country. If the project meets its target, by 2030 the entire national network will become one contiguous set of road works.

Despite the anarchy, we saw surprisingly little evidence of road accidents. However, the statistical reality is stark, with India's annual road fatality rate per 100,000 being over five times higher than the UK's. The reasons are well-acknowledged – road conditions, vehicle maintenance, road user awareness, and traffic enforcement – again, all works in progress.

As one taxi driver candidly admitted, breaking traffic laws comes with a paltry fine, easily circumvented with a few rupees.

Travelling on Indian roads is not for the faint-hearted. It provides an adrenaline-enhanced experience that may test even the bravest of travellers. Understanding what you're letting yourself in for is crucial, and if the chaos proves too much, alternative means of travel might be the wiser choice. In our whimsical reliance on Ganesha, we found ourselves safely guided through the tumultuous seas of Indian roads, and we will be forever grateful to him.

We somehow got to the airport intact and we had suddenly finished our stay in Pune. Three nights in one place was a luxury we didn't surpass anywhere else on our three-week trip.

Devoting an entire chapter to Goa is rather optimistic. Spending little more than twenty-four hours there, we hardly had time to form a first impression, but it left some powerful memories in that brief encounter. Our glimpse of this part of India was always going to be a fleeting one, but as events transpired, we ended up with even less time than we'd planned – time for only the briefest of snapshots.

Goa is India's smallest and most prosperous state. It's about the size of Devon, but it packs an exotic punch. Nestled on the Arabian coast, less than 400 miles south of Mumbai, its 3,702 square kilometres provide a paradise of sandy golden beaches, serene coves, and spice-laden bazaars. As a former Portuguese outpost, Goa's tropical beaches still pulse with a distinctive Portuguese rhythm. The state's rich historical heritage is evident in the charming fusion of Portuguese-era churches and traditional Hindu temples that grace its landscape, creating a unique cultural blend that reflects its colourful past.

While these days Goa's bohemian spirit might not be as 'far-out' as in the 1960s and 1970s, that essence still lingers in pockets like Arambol and Anjuna. Those heady days of full-blown flower power have been gradually replaced by the more subtle embrace of freedom and connection with nature. Think less tie-dye T-shirts and more barefoot strolls on the beach… although you might still find the odd tie-dye if you're lucky. These days, the soul of the place pulsates with a gentle rhythm of mindfulness and a deep connection with the natural world. It's a place where you can shed your inhibitions, embrace your inner peace, and discover a different way of being, one sun-kissed beach and mindful breath at a time. Yoga has blossomed into a defining feature of the area. Studios and retreats sprout like vibrant hibiscus flowers, catering to all levels for both locals and visitors alike. Nick and I only had one night booked for a stopover in Goa. I'd hoped we would have the best part of two days there, just enough to explore some of the UNESCO World Heritage Site churches and take a dip in the Arabian Sea. Things didn't turn out that way.

While we waited patiently in the departure lounge at Pune airport, I scanned the flight information boards for up-to-date news on our flight. Something didn't seem right. Months before our trip, I'd booked our flights to Dabolim airport, near to the coast in Goa. Booking a hotel near to the airport meant we'd minimise our travelling time so we could hit the beach and make the most of our short stopover there.

I could see our flight number on the flight departure board, but the airport code next to it wasn't the one I expected to see. What was happening? Was our flight going somewhere else? Maybe we'd inadvertently bought a couple of Schrodinger flight tickets – we could be going to Dabolim airport, or we might not be. We'd only know when we collapsed the quantum wave function by taking the flight and observing where we landed.

Another waiting passenger reassured us that the flight on the departure board was indeed the one for Goa. I still wasn't convinced, and call me old-fashioned, but I really wanted to go to the airport we'd bought tickets for. Nick's old cartographic skills proved decisive. He looked at the map and solved the mystery – we *were* flying to Goa… but not to the airport I'd booked the tickets for. We were going to Manohar International Airport.

At the boarding gate I questioned the airline staff about our flight, and they assured us everything was fine, suggesting we should continue the discussion with the cabin crew… and please keep moving. Once aboard and strapped in, the charming cabin-crew woman did a nice little side swerve by advising us to contact the company's representative when we arrived.

Arriving 50 kilometres east of the airport we'd bought tickets for, I was hoping the airline would be full of apologies and they'd arrange a speedy taxi transfer for us. Nick was more realistic about our chances, and he was right. The young lady in the airline office, wearing trendy shades, fashionable top and distressed jeans, saw no problem in us being in the wrong place. She told us the airline had to change airports a few months earlier and everyone with tickets had been informed. That put me on the back foot, and I began to wonder if maybe they'd emailed us and I hadn't seen the message? Time to move on, make new plans, and put it all behind us quickly.

Despite the setback, we enjoyed the two-hour taxi ride to our guest house on Bogmalo Beach, on the Vasco da Gama peninsula. Not stressing over the airport mix-up, we savoured the journey, noticing the uncommonly clean vehicles and lower traffic density in Goa. I'm not sure how accurate our driver's tourist guide to the area was, but he told us, 'North Goa is for noisy activity, south Goa is for quiet honeymoon couples.' We were heading for somewhere in the middle… expecting to find lots of noisy active honeymoon couples. With that north–south divide clarified, Nick was quick to quiz our driver on the local licensing arrangements and the availability of wine shops. In India, licensing laws relating to alcohol are typically overseen by the state government's excise department or the state excise commissioner's office. It's a complex and regularly changing situation. Nick may be the only person on the planet who completely understands the situation in every one of India's twenty-eight states and eight Union Territories. He could dominate *Mastermind* with Indian licensing laws as his specialist subject.

Here we saw more of those roadside G20 hoardings, posters and paintings. The 2nd Health Working Group Meeting had been held in Goa a few months earlier, focusing on critical health issues, including India's pharmaceutical sector, which is valued at over $65 billion per year. It's a booming sector and arguably even more important for the Indian economy than Nick's wine shop expenditure. India plays a crucial role in the global supply of generic medicines and has emerged as a world leader in drug manufacturing and research. The Indian pharmaceutical industry was instrumental in the global fight against COVID-19, ramping up production of vaccines and medical supplies, ensuring worldwide availability and affordability. I might owe them thanks myself – the Oxford/AstraZeneca vaccine, one of the most widely used in the UK, had large quantities manufactured by the Serum Institute of India, the world's largest vaccine manufacturer.

We arrived at our guest house, which overlooked the beach, by late afternoon. As the taxi pulled up, we could hear the sound of aircraft landing at the nearby Dabolim airport. An hour later, with the sun touching the horizon and painting the sky an impressionistic tableau of orange and pink, Nick and I were taking a relaxing swim in the calm waters of the Arabian Sea. The surface was as smooth as a mirror, and the sea temperature was as inviting as the proverbial warm bath. It was so relaxing to be lifted slowly by the gentle rhythm of the long ocean rollers, as if we were weightless, and then to be tenderly lowered down again. That's how you melt away travel tribulations. We stayed for about an hour, took some photos, had some photos taken of us, had some more photos taken of us, and then made our way back to the guest house, all of 50 metres away, to change for the evening.

Bogmalo Beach is a quiet little coastal haven with golden sands, calm waters, and swaying palm trees. There are water sports if you want them, but if not you can enjoy leisurely strolls, hang out on the beach and then do what we did – sit by the water's edge and enjoy a seafood cuisine that blends Portuguese technique with Indian flavours. The evocatively named Full Moon restaurant was the perfect place to collapse after a day that hadn't gone completely to plan. This is India – you learn to go with the flow, and who knows, our inconvenience might have been due to my oversight anyway. Cool sea breezes wafted through the open sides of the restaurant, beautiful Indian music accompanied the sound of breaking

Bogmalo Beach, Goa

waves, and World Cup cricket played on the TV. That's not an unpleasant combination.

We sampled the typical Goan fish dishes of cafreal (with a marinade of coriander, mint, green chillies, ginger, and garlic) and xacuti (with a rich and aromatic coconut-based gravy blended with spices such as poppy seeds, fennel, cloves, cinnamon, and others). Washed down with cool Indian beers, both dishes were excellent. Sat at the table next to us, enjoying the playful banter of the friendly restaurant staff, were a couple from Leeds. They told us about their well-tested holiday formula that involved flying directly to the nearby Dabolim airport (we'd all like to do that), taking a couple of weeks to travel around other parts of India, then coming back to Bogmalo Beach for a relaxing few days on the beach before flying home again. Another diner, a single Irish chap, gave us some background information about the village. He was another regular visitor and he seemed torn between telling us how amazing everything was and not wanting too many people to know about what he thought was his secret place.

Nick had one more thing on his mind. On the way back to our guest house, we stopped at a barber's shop, its interior glimmering in the neon-lit street between the boutiques and souvenir shops. It was the very definition of functional, although somehow friendly and welcoming. The skinny guy holding the cut-throat razor to Nick's throat looked about fourteen years old. I was sweating with nervous energy just watching him, but to his credit the young lad did a good job. For the equivalent of £1.50 Nick emerged back into the dark of the night thirty minutes later like a new man – with not a hair on his head, apart from his eyebrows. With Nick's newly shorn head glistening under the stars, Bogmalo Beach cast a calming spell to disperse the stress of the day's travelling. Even when plans go awry, sometimes all it takes is a beautiful beach, some swaying palms, and a plate of fiery xacuti to set things right. We left the golden sands behind, to a background sound of gently breaking waves. Goa left a big impression on us even in the briefest of encounters. The next day, we were set for even more travelling. We'd be on a train for most of the day, ending up in Hospet. Well, that was the plan, but we'd have to see what the travel gods had in mind for us on the day.

Our stopover in Goa had been brief but memorable. Nick and I were heading inland again next and further south. We were going to a place my Lonely Planet guidebook ranks as second only to the Taj Mahal in its list of top tourist sights in India. That's got to be something special, although three months prior to arriving in southern India I'm ashamed to say I'd never heard of it. The UNESCO World Heritage Site of Hampi is situated almost in the middle of the country and about 1,400 kilometres (about 870 miles) north of its southern tip. The centuries-old remains of the city of Vijayanagara lie exposed over a vast dusty plateau, their grandeur still formidable despite being reduced to sun-bleached ruins.

But first we had to get to Hampi from Goa, and that involved re-acquainting ourselves with Indian Railways for ten hours. After our previous trip to India, we were huge fans of the railways, so it was something we were looking forward to. If you get your timetable and seat reservations right, you're rewarded with an inexpensive slow tour through the Indian countryside with food and drink, good company (usually) and room to take a nap if you need to catch up on some sleep, which I normally do. Getting your seat reservation right, in our experience, involves booking tickets in the AC2 carriage class.

India's rail network is world famous. It pulsates day and night, carrying more passengers than any other network in the world. Nearly 80,000 miles of steel track and over 7,000 stations allow passengers and goods to reach the furthest corners of the subcontinent. The official Indian Railways website (www.indianrail.gov.in) is your go-to place for nearly all journeys, but hunting down tickets for some routes, like the toy trains to Shimla and Darjeeling, can require a bit of extra detective work. Planning your route can be fun, and I'm sure there are people out there who love it. In my experience, a session with the Indian Railways website requires great perseverance and almost infinite patience. With practice, it's possible to find the routes you want and the times that are most convenient for you. You can then book the tickets online from the comfort of your own home, pay for them by international bankers card and print the tickets to take with you. The payment might be challenging, but I can reassure you there is a combination of clicks and windows that makes it possible. Anyone who's mastered the Rubik's cube should be fine, but if you have to, you can do as I did and send an email to someone at Indian Railways who will clear the mystery for you – good luck!

In terms of seat choice, there are many to choose from and it's a good idea to know what to expect from each one. There are websites that can help to explain this in great detail. For overnight journeys or long day trips like the one we were about to take from Goa, the AC2 cabins became our favourite. They are popular with middle-class Indian families and provide bunks in cosy air-conditioned compartments with blankets and pillows. They even have curtains. AC3 is its slightly more crowded cousin, providing a similar experience at an even more affordable price. For those seeking luxury, but still comparably cheap by European standards, try the premium trains with AC1 cabins. They are a bit like first or business class, with spacious seats, 'in-flight' meals, and panoramic views. Many Indian rail users end up in the Sleeper class, a bustling and earthy microcosm of everyday India that pulsates with energy, chatter, and perspiration. This is where you travel with the masses, without air conditioning or bedding – it's just you, the carriage, and lots of hot (mostly) Indian people. But that experience – windows flung open to the countryside's rhythm, bunks shared with strangers, and the enticing aroma of chai mingling with local chatter – is an immersive plunge into the medley of Indian life, not for the faint of heart but an undeniably authentic experience. For that one, be sure to pack your sense of adventure and a big smile.

Francis, whose guest house we were staying in at Bogmalo Beach, Goa, took us into town first thing in the morning, in good time to meet our train at Vasco da Gama station. The weather was warm and sunny, but then it nearly always is. Francis dropped us off at his favourite bakery so we could pick up some breakfast and a few treats for our journey. We soon found our seats on the train (they were actually seven-foot-long benches) and after pulling out of the station only fifteen minutes late, we settled in.

Leaving the coastal charm of Goa, the train heads inland and due east, slowly climbing up into the Western Ghats. The vegetation changes from agricultural to increasingly dense woodland – gradually morphing into emerald-green hills, cascading waterfalls, and dense tropical forests. The Ghats provide another sensory experience, with fragrant plants, tall trees sprinkled with blossoms, and the distant sounds of nature. That experience is quite 'in your face' when you're trundling along at only 20 miles per hour, sitting in the doorway of the train with the door wide open and dangling your feet outside with nothing between you and the passing scenery. It was a great way to travel – in between reading a book about yoga and taking the occasional forty winks. Nick and I took it in turns to visit the train door, while the other one kept an eye on the bags. It was on one such foray that Nick bumped into Pete and Hilary from Salisbury… our first Brits since leaving Heathrow! Touring around India you meet surprisingly few fellow Brits, even in the tourist spots. I recall a long conversation with Hilary about cracking the code to buy tickets on the Indian Railways website, and another one in which we discussed favourite Indian dishes. I wrote one of Pete's pearls of wisdom in my diary, so I must have thought it was significant at the time. Reading it again now I can see that it truly was. He thought the biggest difference between north and south India is the lack of cow pats in the south.

An hour and a half into our journey, we entered the verdant embrace of the Bhagwan Mahavir Wildlife Sanctuary, home to the Molem National Park. At night, if you're lucky, you might catch sight of prowling Bengal tigers, leopards, and black panthers… but not much chance of that on a clanking train in the middle of the day. The train track slowly snakes higher into the Ghats, carefully hugging the contours to maintain a comfortable incline. Then, drawn by an unseen force into one of those magnificent switchback loops, the train gave us a front-row seat to the awe-inspiring Dudhsagar Falls. They rank as the fifth-highest waterfall in India, and that's another good reason to travel by train – you wouldn't get that view at 30,000 feet.

You hear the roar of the falls before you see them, a breathtaking cascade of foaming white water plunging 100 feet down bulging grey basalt cliffs, right next to the railway. The total height of the falls is over 1,000 feet. The falls weren't at their peak when we saw them (monsoon is May to September), but the display was more than enough to justify their name, which translates to 'Sea of Milk'. And of course, being India, there has to be a legend to explain a perfectly good topographical feature. Here we can thank a local princess. She is said to have bathed in the crystal-clear waters at the top of the mountain, then, like most of us after bathing, she quenched her thirst with sweetened milk from a golden jug… and hence the milky look of the tumbling waters.

Transitioning to agricultural plains again as we continued eastwards from the mountains, the earthy brown and green shades of the landscape were punctuated by vibrant green rice fields and golden sugarcane. As we journeyed further inland, we came across increasing amounts of coconut and banana plantations. Rural settlements dotted the horizon, and occasionally we'd get a closeup view of one as we slowly trundled through. Little children would sometimes shout and clap excitedly as if it was the first time they'd set eyes on a train. Crossing bridges over meandering rivers added to the enchantment of the journey, and then approaching Hospet, the Deccan Plateau slowly unveils its rocky grandeur. We arrived in Hospet, near Hampi, almost ten hours after boarding the train in Goa. We were an hour and a half late, but somehow it didn't matter, and the time hadn't dragged. I'd had at least four hours sleep and was beginning to come back to earth after the flight out to India and a few long days that had battered my senses and energy levels.

A tuk-tuk delivered us from the station to the Malligi Hotel in central Hospet. We'd planned our stay to coincide with Diwali, and not to disappoint us, the locals greeted us in the street outside the hotel with an impressive display of minor ordinance. The strategy adopted by the teenagers of Hospet (and everywhere else in India it seems) is to buy the biggest box of fireworks the shop will sell you, put the entire box on the pavement somewhere inconvenient, and then throw a match in. Rockets could be fired along the street just as easily as up into the sky. I'm sure the fireworks that greeted us when we arrived at the hotel, masquerading as stun-grenades, were the sort banned in the UK several decades ago. Fantastic – that was quite an entrance.

After getting showered, changed, and waiting a while for the ringing in our ears to subside, Nick and I headed down to reception to get a recommendation for somewhere to eat. But this is India. Instead, a very elegantly dressed man approached us and asked, 'Would you like to attend a puja…? You will be our guests… Will cost you nothing, sirs.'

Well, you would, wouldn't you? Puja, or pooja, is a ritualistic worship practice performed by Hindus, Buddhists, and Jains. It signifies reverence, the honouring of deities, and the spiritual celebration of events, which in our case, was Diwali. Still inside the hotel, and trusting our safety to Ganesha, we were escorted up some stairs. We seemed to be the first to arrive in a highly decorated function room. That felt slightly awkward, but we embraced the unknown. On a stage that stretched across one end of the room stood a magnificent four-foot-tall model of Lakshmi, the Hindu goddess of wealth, fortune, prosperity, and good luck. She was depicted as a stunningly beautiful woman radiating warmth and serenity. Seated on a throne surrounded by an elaborately decorated stage adorned with giant lotus leaves, palm trees, and elephants, she seemed to hold court.

Two gentlemen in colourful traditional Indian attire sat cross-legged in front of Lakshmi. A small table beside them overflowed with offerings of food and flowers. One of the men, holding a microphone, chanted passages from a holy book, while the other occasionally cast handfuls of rice in Lakshmi's direction. The gentle clinking of the rice and the melodic chanting filled the air with a sense of peace. Four beautiful women in brightly coloured saris stood gracefully to one side, offering approving nods and bows to the proceedings.

As the ritual continued on stage, we were ushered towards rows of seats that could accommodate at least a hundred guests. We were handed delicious coconut milkshakes as we settled in, and soon more people began to file in, filling the room with a gentle buzz. After about twenty minutes, the chanting ceased. By then, the room had filled with around sixty well-dressed individuals, who appeared to belong to the middle and upper classes of Hospet society.

When the audience rose and moved towards the stage, we followed suit. We took our turn to grab a handful of rice, walked up to Lakshmi, and sprinkled it over her while bowing in reverence. The air was thick with the sweet scent of incense and the fragrance of the floral offerings. The ceremony concluded with everyone enjoying a generous buffet and engaging in lively conversation. Many attendees seemed to know each other, creating a warm, familiar atmosphere that reminded me of a congregation meeting outside their church after communion on a Sunday back home. I eventually found myself in conversation with an immaculately dressed man who turned out to be the son of the hotel owner. In impeccable English, he explained that the puja was an annual celebration much enjoyed in Hospet during Diwali. Each year the hotel opens its doors to the people of the town, welcoming them to celebrate and share food together.

The highlight of the evening had been the opportunity for everyone to make an 'Akshata' offering to Lakshmi – a sacred ritual involving the sprinkling of a consecrated mix of uncooked rice grains and turmeric, symbolising prayers for good luck, prosperity, and the blessings of the goddess. Initially, I found it curious that a goddess would be in charge of wealth and prosperity; it seemed an unusual portfolio for a deity. However, I soon learnt that Lakshmi also oversees well-being, peace, harmony, and freedom from hunger. It's complicated. Indeed, the whole Hindu deity-worshipper relationship is far more nuanced than one might first realise. As explained in the previous chapter, Hindus perceive the divine as living within their earthly representations, making day-to-day connections both real and deeply sought after. We thanked our hosts for their generous hospitality and wondered what other good fortune Lakshmi might bring our way over the next two days in Hospet.

CHAPTER 4

JAI SHRI RAM!

Spread over a vast plateau of undulating rocky terrain that spans about 26 square kilometres (10 square miles) of central southern India, Hampi is an archaeological site of profound significance. The *New York Times* once had it as second on their list of must-see places in the world. During the 16th century, half a million people lived on that dusty plain, in the richest city in India… it was the second-largest city in the world!

Nowadays, it's like a drive-through archaeological theme park or open-air museum. Wide expanses of parched landscape are interrupted by small rusty-coloured hills, rocky outcrops, and massive boulders, some balanced improbably on narrow pedestals. The mighty Tungabhadra River winds a watery streak through the rocky terrain, sustaining the scattered palm groves and paddy fields that decorate the scene with splashes of jade and emerald green.

Let's consider the geology. Nick always does. The Hampi plain lies on the Deccan Plateau, a geographical region that encompasses a vast area spanning several states including Maharashtra, Karnataka, Telangana, and Andhra Pradesh. It is near the Deccan Traps, an extensive and dense series of basaltic lava flows which originated from massive volcanic eruptions that occurred around 66 million years ago during the late Cretaceous period. Over millions of years, successive layers of lava accumulated, forming thick basalt deposits that make up much of the Deccan Plateau's bedrock. They comprise one of the largest volcanic regions on the planet. The presence of the Deccan Traps contributes to the unique geological formations found in and around Hampi. Over millions of years, the granite has been eroded, firstly underground, then later, after being exposed by gradual uplift, by sun, wind, and occasional rain. The process has produced features known as inselbergs (isolated hills rising abruptly from the surrounding plains), as well as vast areas of rocky and rugged terrain.

Well over 1,000 sun-baked temples, shrines, royal monuments, and other archaeological remnants lie scattered across this unearthly landscape… silent witnesses to its long history. Some sources suggest the number could be closer to 4,000, but with ongoing excavations and new discoveries constantly being made, it's a moving feast. They're going to need a bigger museum.

Hampi is more than just a landscape of spectacular ruins; it's a place steeped in deep mythological significance. Revered as the birthplace of Hanuman, the beloved monkey god, Hampi is intimately connected to the legendary events of the *Ramayana*, one of Hinduism's most important epics. This sacred ground is where the epic's heroic exploits are said to have unfolded. Yet, it is the archaeological wonders of this UNESCO World Heritage Site that draw most visitors today. The remarkable ruins, now a backdrop for tourists and their selfies, were once the thriving heart of the ancient Vijayanagara Empire. What makes Hampi truly extraordinary isn't just the impressive physical remnants, but the profound stories and rich history that they embody.

The area is rich in natural resources and has been inhabited since prehistoric times. Excavations have unearthed Buddhist panels made of limestone, dating back to the 1st–2nd centuries AD.

Hampi rose to prominence in 1336, however, when Harihara I and his brother Bukka Raya I, founders of the Vijayanagara Empire, chose it as the location for their new capital city. They ordered it to be constructed from local granite, burnt bricks, and lime mortar. Those founding fathers, and subsequent Vijayanagara kings, were passionate about their religion and art, and lavished vast sums on the city's architecture and the contents of its temples and buildings. The empire flourished as a major trading power for two centuries under four different dynasties, helped by its control over key ports like Goa, Nagapattinam, and Mangalore, and its favourable position astride important trading routes. The city served as a hub for Western traders acquiring goods from Southeast Asia, the Persian Gulf, and the Red Sea. Horses were imported from the West and exchanged for Chinese silk, ceramics, and other precious items. The city thrived on the trade of spices, precious stones, and valuable metals, particularly silver. Its rulers became enormously rich, none more so than the city's fifth ruler, Krishnadevaraya. He was an exceptional king, who arrived at the right place at the right time – a winning combination that all aspiring empire rulers would be wise to emulate. During the 16th century, Krishnadevaraya led the Vijayanagara Empire to become the strongest force in southern India, helping to resource his penchant for architectural extravagance and lavish decoration. Under his rule the city reached its zenith. Domingo Paes, a Portuguese traveller who visited Vijayanagara, said, 'What I saw... seemed to me as large as Rome, and very beautiful to the sight... The people in this city are countless in number, so much so that I do not wish to write it down for fear it should be thought fabulous.'

But the travellers who marvelled at its exquisite temples and opulent palaces also brought the city to the attention of less benevolent admirers. Eventually, the temptation was too much for the neighbouring Deccan Sultanates (a good name for a Dire Straits tribute band). They wanted the city's riches for themselves, and they got their way after a series of bloody invasions. The Battle of Talikota in 1565 was decisive and resulted in the ultimate downfall of the city of Vijayanagara. The empire crumbled. A once-magnificent capital lay in tatters, but its new owners didn't seem to view the place as a going concern. They did their plundering and went home, leaving the ancient city in dusty ruins. When the Mughals arrived in the early 17th century, there was little left of Vijayanagara worth restoring. A few small communities continued living there, but the Mughals looked elsewhere to establish their centres of power; places such as Aurangabad and Hyderabad. Vijayanagara had become a glorious chapter in Indian history.

Nowadays, the vast scorched plateau of Hampi is home to countless monuments that echo that illustrious past, including palaces, forts, memorial structures, temples, shrines, pillared halls, baths, gateways… and not forgetting the Elephants' Stables.

But back to the start of our two full days to see the sights of Hampi. Two days seems a lot of time in one place for Nick and me, but it wasn't nearly enough, there is just so much to see. We packed a lot into the time we had, though. To make life easy, we hired a tuk-tuk driver for our two days.

Looking back, our driver, Asha, played an astute tactical marketing ploy when he first spotted Nick and me arriving at the railway station in Hospet, the nearest large town to Hampi. His meagre charge to take us to our hotel, severely undercutting the competition, could only have been a break-even fare at best. When we saw him the following morning, however, outside our hotel, we already knew him and we liked him, so it was a simple decision to choose him again. His meagre loss-leader fare from the station the night before had earned him another two full days of business.

Asha was in his late thirties, dressed very simply in a saffron robe and sandals, and was a husband and father. He told us, in fairly good English, that he was halfway through several weeks of a strict Hindu ritual that sounded similar to Ramadan for Muslims. It involved specific dietary restrictions and dedicating long periods, outside working hours, to meditation. The self-imposed constraints also included sleeping each night in a remote rural temple, rather than at home with his family. If he was tired or undernourished, he showed no signs of it. He was a human dynamo, telling us countless stories about Hampi and repeatedly brightening our day with his huge beaming smile. Using Asha's guidance, we tried to get round most of the 'must-see' sights of Hampi on our first day, leaving some of the highlights that were further afield for our second day.

That first day was brutal, relentlessly ticking off site after site around the central part of Hampi. Instead of providing you with a long list of the places we visited, which you could easily find for yourself in the guidebooks, I'll concentrate on a few highlights that stood out for Nick and me. To get the best from your visit, find yourselves a good driver/guide and be prepared for lots of walking. We walked over 15 miles each day we were in Hampi. And don't forget the water, and a map. Oh, and maybe a third day would be a good idea. But it's all worth it, it is a remarkable place to visit.

Appropriately, Asha began our tour by taking us to the imposing Talargatta Gate. Nowadays, it's slightly rickety-looking, but still an impressive sight considering its great age. Like my left knee. The stone archway marked the gateway to the once-mighty Vijayanagara City. We could almost hear the rumble of royal chariots and the sound of marching soldiers as they passed triumphantly through the arch on the road in front of us.

Delving deeper into the heart of the UNESCO-designated area, we reached the enormous Vittala Temple Complex, home to the magnificent stone Vijaya Vittala Temple. Vittala is the name of the deity worshipped at the temple, but perhaps I should briefly explain more about that.

In Hinduism, the universe is inhabited by a multitude of deities, each fulfilling specific roles within the religion's mythology and practices. At the very top is Brahman, the ultimate, formless, and all-encompassing reality or power. Beneath Brahman are three principal gods known as the Trimurti: Brahma, the creator of the universe; Vishnu, the preserver who maintains cosmic order (often descending to Earth in various forms); and Shiva, the destroyer who facilitates the cycle of creation by bringing about necessary endings, allowing the universe to begin anew.

Hindu stories often have multiple versions, and further complexity arises from variations in the names and spellings of the deities involved. Different regions of India and various schools of Hinduism may emphasise particular interpretations, which can make it rather intricate for visitors to grasp. In our temple in Hampi, worshippers venerate the god Vittala. Some consider Vittala to be a unique earthly manifestation of Vishnu, while others associate him with Krishna, another well-known avatar of Vishnu.

The Vittala Temple complex spans a vast area, encompassing numerous shrines, halls, courtyards, and structures, each with its own mysteries and stories. With so much to see and comprehend, Nick and I decided to splurge on a local guide to show us around. The centrepiece of the complex is the richly ornate Vijaya Vittala Temple, built from local granite. Adorned with mythological figures and floral motifs, it remains breathtakingly beautiful despite its age. Surrounding a central plinth are fifty-six musical pillars, sometimes called SaReGaMa pillars because of the musical notes they produce (sa-re-ga-ma is the Indian classical music scale, like do-re-mi-fa in Western music). When struck with a thumb, the stone pillars emit sounds like ringing bells. Years of overenthusiastic tour guides demonstrating this have led to a ban on tapping the pillars. Our guide described how, hundreds of years ago, the pillars were used to provide music for lavish ceremonies. Then, making sure the security guard wasn't watching, he couldn't resist using his thumbs to tap out a quick Hampi indo-jazz rap on his vertical stone xylophone.

Also in the complex is the Mahanavami Dibba, a raised platform used for royal audiences and religious ceremonies. The Kalyana Mantapa is a pillared pavilion originally built for marriage ceremonies and royal events. And the star of the show is the Stone Chariot. Boasting dimensions of 13 metres in length, 7 metres in width, and 10 metres in height, the remarkable structure was originally carved from a single piece of granite in the 16th century. King Krishnadevaraya is the man responsible for its creation, reportedly inspired by the Konark Sun Temple chariot he encountered during a battle in Odisha (another UNESCO World Heritage Site on the shores of the Bay of Bengal). I can just imagine him in the heat of battle spotting the Konark stone chariot and stopping to make a note: 'Must get the guys to carve me one of those out of solid granite when I get home.' The Stone Chariot of the

The Stone Chariot, Hampi

Vijaya Vittala Temple served as a shrine dedicated to Garuda, Lord Vishnu's vehicle, and has become an iconic symbol of Hampi and its glorious past. It symbolises the artistic perfection and architectural prowess of the Vijayanagara Empire, and its image continues to grace the Indian 50-rupee currency note.

Moving on, we admired the Hazara Rama Temple, where intricate carvings adorn the temple walls. The carvings represent the Ramayana story told in stone, with war scenes, triumphs, and dancing figures, illustrating the richness of Hindu culture and traditions.

Demonstrating the sheer opulence of the empire, the nearby King's Balance is the remains of a stone-framed weighing scale used to measure the monarch's worth in gold, gems, or other precious commodities. Moving next to the ornate architecture of the Queen's Bath, we had a glimpse into the extravagant lifestyle of the city's royalty.

Asha took us to a small hill off the beaten track where we had a spectacular view over the sun-baked plain. In the foreground was the Nobleman's Quarters, the residential area that once accommodated the nobility and high-ranking officials of the Vijayanagara Empire. Nearby, the imposing King's Audience Hall served as a place for the king to hold court and conduct official meetings. Its typically ornate carvings, pillars, and layout emphasised the grandeur and authority of the king.

We'd been looking forward to seeing the Elephants' Stables, which are just what the name suggests. A set of eleven were used to house the royal elephants of the Vijayanagara Empire and by good fortune they've survived better than most buildings in the old city. They were no ordinary stables, of course. The terraced row of eleven huge stable buildings with domed roofs were designed with a very stylish blend of Islamic and Hindu architectural elements, and decorated with intricate carvings. Built to show off the multicultural influences prevalent during the Vijayanagara period, they weren't just functional buildings to house animals, they were a statement of the empire's wealth and power.

As the afternoon wore on, Asha took us to the archaeological museum in Hospet, near to our hotel. It was surprisingly quiet, but Asha told us that few tourists realise it's even there.

By now, your eyes are probably glazing over with ancient relic fatigue. But if you think I've mentioned a lot of sites, I've spared you the descriptions of over thirty more temples, palaces, buildings, or monuments that we crammed into our long day touring around the Hampi site. Asha certainly knew his stuff, and I don't know how we'd have managed without him. He got his timing just right by ending our first sightseeing day at the Virupaksha Temple, with its magnificent tower, just as the sun dipped below the horizon, casting long shadows on the ancient ruins. Often called Pampapathi Temple, the Virupaksha Temple is a prominent landmark in Hampi, and one of its 'big-hitter' tourist attractions. With an uninterrupted history dating back to the 7th century, it is one of the most sacred temples in India. The spectacular tower, visible from many miles around, stands approximately 50 metres (164 feet) tall, resembling a giant extended pyramid adorned with ornate carvings. Real-life troops of macaque monkeys clamber acrobatically over the sides and dangle dangerously from the top.

Adding to its spiritual significance and cultural charm, the temple features its own resident elephant, Lakshmi, who plays a ceremonial role during religious rituals and festivals. Despite the many other attractions of the temple, it was Lakshmi who seemed to be the biggest draw for visitors when we arrived — just in time to see her enjoying her early-evening meal.

By the end of the day, it was hard to avoid slipping into that slightly punch-drunk state that you get into when you've spent a few hours too many in a museum… a combination of information and sensory overload mixed with tiredness, overheating, thirst, and hunger. Fortunately, the places we saw were extraordinary – but you're still left a little stunned by the sheer scale of the site and the overwhelming numbers of temples, monuments, and artefacts.

Back at our hotel, we were more than ready for our evening meal by the time we went down to the restaurant. Lacking the brain capacity to think, I asked the server for a recommendation.

'I'd like something vegetarian please, and not too spicy,' I said.

Back came the answer in flash, 'Butter chicken'.

It was probably the way I worded it, but I was too tired to get into a discussion. Washed down with a Kingfisher beer, it was absolutely delicious.

After a good night's sleep, we were raring to go again for our second full day's sightseeing in Hampi. Our first stop though was to meet one of Asha's friends… the barber. In his modest but friendly little shop I had all my beard shaved off, a haircut, and a twenty-minute head massage, for the equivalent of £3 – and most of that was the tip. Our schedule for the day involved fewer stops than the previous day, some longer tuk-tuk rides, more walking, and a boat ride.

First, we were heading for Anjanadri Hill, along some beautiful little lanes through bright green paddy fields and lush plantations of bananas, coconuts, and sugarcane. This was a relatively lush area, kept that way by the Tungabhadra River, its tributaries and a network of irrigation channels. At places along the roadside verges large sheets of tarpaulin had been laid out and covered in a thin layer of rice. The rice had been picked from nearby fields and was drying in the sun. Occasionally we'd see someone barefooted, walking up and down the large squares of tarpaulin, kicking the rice around to help it dry. We saw other people bagging the dried rice to be collected and taken to nearby stores. In some fields, ripe sugarcane stalks lay freshly cut, awaiting carts to haul them to nearby buildings. There, the husks would be stripped of their contents and left in enormous piles before being burnt.

Anjanadri Hill was just 3 miles from our hotel in Hospet. As we drove further from the town, the vegetation grew gradually thinner and then quite sparse. Our route took us through a vast area of open land near the scattered settlement of Bukkasagara – to what, for Nick, was one of the highlights of our entire three-week trip.

Continuing through a barren-looking landscape of thin soils and sparse vegetation, we spotted some people a couple of hundred metres away from the road. Asha told us they were quarrying granite. Nick's eyes lit up and he immediately requested a pit stop. We walked over the crest of a gently domed hill and then stopped abruptly in our tracks. Before us lay a sight that might have remained largely unchanged for hundreds of years.

The thin surface layer of soil had been cleared away to expose the raw granite base rock underneath. It seemed to stretch for miles ahead in a large dome-like geological formation. Immediately in front of us, a rough circle of about 100 metres diameter had been hacked out of the landscape to form a shallow quarry. A handful of men, dressed in nothing more than flimsy shorts and vests and wearing flip-flops were carving blocks of granite out of the hillside using hand tools. Health and Safety considerations didn't seem to be a priority; this was no place for frivolities like gloves, ear defenders, steel-capped footwear, or safety glasses.

There was no machinery in sight anywhere – unless you count one clapped-out moped, lying on its side. From where we stood, the exposed grey granite rock of the surface descended in 2-metre steps, like contour lines, to the floor of the basin-shaped quarry. In places there was only one step down from the top surface, in others it stepped down in three layers of terrace. We watched for a while mesmerised by the scene. Nick eventually got chatting with one quarryman to find out more about the methods he was using.

Using nothing more complicated than hand chisels, hammers of various sizes, and wedges, the workers were carefully carving out rectangular blocks from the solid rock face. We watched as they hammered short metal spikes into the granite in rows, spacing them according to the size of the blocks they needed. Continuous pounding with a sledgehammer along the line of spikes eventually caused a fracture and a strip of granite could be prised away. It was gruelling work in punishing temperatures. We saw no refrigerated drinks coolers for the guys to congregate around while they talked about the previous night's game, this year's performance appraisal interviews, or Meera from accounts.

We were exhausted just watching. It wasn't just brute force being used, although there was plenty of that. The workers were being very precise with their measurements, and the force they applied, to ensure that the blocks were cut to just the right size and shape without any unnecessary cracking. Once cut to a variety of shapes and sizes, the blocks were stacked, to be transported away using carts or small trucks for use on construction sites or sent elsewhere for further processing. Who knows, some blocks might end up as worktops in little shops in Vakola, in suburban Mumbai.

We walked on, wandering gradually further from the road. Asha must have thought we'd deserted him. Drawn by loud booming noises further over the brow of the hill, we went to investigate – by then we must have been a kilometre from the road. There, where vast expanses of flat granite were exposed at the surface, we saw a completely different quarrying technique. Small fires had been lit using brushwood to heat specific areas of the rock. The rock expands unevenly because of the heat, causing natural fractures to form. The quarrymen then used sledgehammers to strike the heated areas, to further fracture the rock. The sound boomed out around the landscape and echoed hauntingly into the distance like the explosive exhalations of a slumbering subterranean volcano, threatening to awaken from its restless slumber.

It looked like incredibly hard work. With the repeated heating and pounding, the layers of granite eventually separate, like exfoliating layers of an onion. The separated layers were being broken down into smaller pieces using hand tools, and the granite piled into heaps of similar-sized pieces before being removed from the quarry. These un-mechanised techniques must have been used like this, unchanged, for centuries. It wasn't hard to imagine a similar scene in the 14th century, when the original builders of Vijayanagara came looking for the granite blocks to build their temples and palaces.

Nick and I were glad to find Asha again when we eventually got back to the road. He was horizontal in the back of his tuk-tuk, his legs hanging out of the side, catching up with some sleep.

Anjanadri Hill was not far away by now and we could see it standing out clearly from the surrounding plain. You can see the hill for miles around with its white zigzag of steps leading up one side. The whitewashed temple on the summit gleamed like a lighthouse in the bright morning sun. The temple is dedicated to Hanuman, the monkey warrior god. He is a central figure in Hindu mythology, particularly in the epic Ramayana. Hanuman's mother was called Anjana, who was an Apsara (a celestial nymph)... But let's leave that one there. The significant thing, as far as local hill naming is concerned, was that Hanuman was born to Anjana, and therefore, he was also known as Anjaneya. This means his birthplace is sometimes referred to as Anjaneya Hill – or sometimes just Hanuman Hill.

Nick hardly had time to flick back through his newly acquired collection of hundreds of granite quarrying images before we arrived at the hill. Asha dropped us off at a crowded section of road at the base of the stairway that winds its way to the top. Getting to the top by foot is the only option and there are 700 steps. There are no tickets or payments required, you just turn up and start climbing.

There was quite a bustling crowd of visitors swarming around a handful of stalls selling clothes, snacks, and cool drinks on the roadside at the base of the hill. A little lane, flanked by more colourful stalls, led towards the hill. A few stalls had mechanical contraptions into which the owner fed sticks of sugarcane and delicious juice trickled out of the side. We tried some to boost our hydration and energy levels. It was surprisingly refreshing and nothing like as sweet as we were expecting. Asha had disappeared by now, presumably to drum up some more tuk-tuk business, leaving us to toil in the heat for the next three hours.

When the short lane ended, a flight of whitewashed steps took over, taking pilgrims and other visitors upwards to the temple at the top of the hill. We were well stocked with water supplies but felt a bit underdressed compared to other people around us, many of whom were wearing white and bright orange/saffron clothing. Not to look more out of place than we needed to be, we bought a couple of orange scarves and immediately felt part of the collective pilgrimage experience.

As we approached the steps, we squinted against the November sun, sweat already beading on our foreheads despite a gentle breeze.

Surprisingly, we were both sensible enough to have hats on and, fortunately, most of the way up, the steps were roofed to give intrepid climbers respite from the sun.

There was a party atmosphere on the lower sections of the steps, with groups of excited devotees chanting, singing, and laughing in excited anticipation. People coming down were more subdued, until they saw Nick and me of course, when many of them had to stop, and stop us, for a photo. We might be athletes with film-star looks, but two pensioners on a day out don't normally get that kind of celebrity treatment back in Britain.

Pilgrims of all ages huffed and puffed their way up and down the steps. Some climbed with quiet determination, faces etched with concentration. Others chatted excitedly, the sound of their voices supplemented by the gentle tinkling of little hand bells. The air hummed with anticipation, incense mingling with the earthy scent of ancient stone and the less romantic earthy scent of perspiration.

We heard an almost constant refrain of 'Jai Shri Ram'. It's a common Hindu chant that means 'Hail Lord Rama'. The chant signifies devotion and reverence towards Lord Rama, a central figure in Hindu mythology, and an avatar of the Hindu god Vishnu. Singing the chant is used as a form of spiritual affirmation or celebration, particularly among devotees on their way to the temple on top of Anjanadri Hill. In Hindu mythology, Hanuman is deeply devoted to Lord Rama and is often depicted as chanting or repeating the name of Lord Rama himself. By chanting 'Jai Shri Ram', pilgrims are indirectly praising Hanuman's devotion to Lord Rama and honouring their inseparable bond.

A group of very enthusiastic teenage lads took great pleasure in explaining this to us, and their excitement knew no bounds when we joined in the chants with them. A father just ahead of us on the path was very patiently teaching his young toddler how to sing the chant, syllable by syllable. Eventually the boy got it and everyone in earshot burst into applause... and then into even more chanting of 'Jai Shri Ram'.

The path snaked its way up the rocky face of the hill, quite steep in places but no challenge to experienced mountain people like Nick and me. Having to stop for regular selfies was a good excuse for us to catch our breath – although we could easily have kept going had we wanted to. Each turn in the path revealed a fresh scene: families sharing precious water from a communal jug, saffron-clad sadhus lost in deep meditation, and mischievous monkeys swinging through the branches. Laughter, chanting, and whispered prayers danced on the wind, which was gentle and cooling, and very welcome.

After an hour of steady climbing, punctuated by regular photo stops, we finally emerged onto the small, sun-drenched summit plateau, standing over 1,600 feet above sea level. We added our shoes to the hundreds of others being tended to by the shoe minder; it was like the mosh pit at a Sandie Shaw gig – for those old enough to remember.

The Hanuman Temple, with its gleaming whitewashed facade, stood proudly in the midday sun, overlooking the vast expanse of the Hampi plain. A bright orange flag flapped gently in the breeze above the temple. Glorious panoramic vistas unfolded in every direction. Lush valleys, carpeted in emerald green, threaded through the dusty plain that was dotted with clusters of terracotta-roofed houses. Randomly placed clumps of bright green paddy fields and coconut tree plantations stretched towards the horizon.

The mighty Tungabhadra River snaked through the land, glinting like a silver thread.

Looking at the Hampi ruins on the plain below you can see why the Vijayanagara kings chose this area for the capital of their empire. The rugged, rocky mountains that framed the horizon would have given their secluded plain defensive protection and the powerful Tungabhadra River would have provided water, transport, and another defensive barrier.

Nick and I joined maybe a hundred other visitors at the summit, although there can be thousands per day during the peak season and at festival times. Generations of pilgrims, spanning across ages and cultures, sought their own personal connection with the divine. The youngest, barely toddlers, clung to their parents' hands, wide-eyed with wonder. The oldest, their faces almost as etched with time as mine, moved more slowly but with unwavering faith and determination.

We went into the temple to pay our respects and benefit from the cool of the shade. To one side of the temple, in a small walled compound from which there were fabulous views, five women and a man were processing an enormous pile of coconuts. They were methodically breaking them open to extract the coconut water for offerings in the temple. Also near the temple entrance stood a weathered tree, considered sacred and dedicated to Hanuman. Devotees left offerings of saffron scarves, flowers, and coconuts wrapped in orange scarves. One particularly long withered branch stretched wearily out towards a metal archway that contained a huge brass bell. The scene was quite something and the area swarmed with people eager to get a photo of the bell, the view, the tree… and themselves.

A short distance from the temple we found some shade near to a building in which pilgrims could eat. A kitchen was at one end of the seating area and the cook made regular trips in and out of the building as she prepared food. She had propped some washed dishes up against the walls outside to dry in the sun. The local monkeys thought this was too much of an opportunity and every time the cook came out and was distracted, two or three of them would dash into the kitchen and emerge seconds later carrying bags of crisps, biscuits, or whatever else they could find. The cook would then return, shouting loudly and waving her arms to send the monkeys scurrying. This was superb entertainment for a group of little children that was watching – and a couple of elderly British chaps.

We strolled roughly 50 metres to a sign that read, 'sunset spot'. When I say strolled, it was more of a controlled mincing dash. It was like a high-speed traverse over hot coals, as the exposed rock beneath our bare feet felt near to melting point. Remarkably, we completed the dash without requiring medical evacuation. Our fortunate outcome, and unscathed feet, owed much to the Leidenfrost effect. Upon contact with the scorching rock, a thin layer of sweat on our skin instantly vaporised, forming a protective steam barrier that minimised heat transfer to our feet. Additionally, due to the intense heat, and our lack of bravery, our feet spent minimal time in direct contact with the red-hot rock surface.

We took some more photos and sat quietly for a while, taking in the views and considering the significance of the location, before starting our slow walk down again. The climb to the Hanuman Temple on Anjanadri Hill may not have been the most technically challenging, but the magic of the place, the shared experience, the breathtaking views, the palpable faith of those around us would stay long in the memory, or as long as a pensioner's memory will allow. I still have the photos, and writing about it is good insurance against the day those memories begin to fade.

One advantage of being driven around by Asha for two days was that he knew some great places to stop for lunch. Eating simple but delicious Indian food off palm leaf plates with the locals was a special treat. After lunch on day two of our Hampi adventure we thought long and hard whether we really wanted to go for a ride in a coracle on the river, which was what Asha suggested for us next. It would only last forty-five minutes but it felt a bit of a touristy thing to do – we are more adventurer traveller types. But then again, we reasoned, we might never be back again, and being paddled along while we lay back relaxing, with the water lapping gently on the hull of the boat – well, that was quite a nice thought. OK, we'd be tourists.

It was money well spent. Our paddler, Vikram, was an excellent guide and a strong oarsman. The entire experience was very relaxing. There were half a dozen coracles hauled out on the side of the river when we arrived at the site where you hire the boats, and once the negotiations were complete, Vikram dragged his boat over to the water's edge for Nick and me to get aboard. The boat was about 3 metres in diameter and could apparently seat six at a push. It was built from a circular frame made from bamboo and thin wooden strips, covered with a waterproof material which looked like tar-coated canvas. Handles, seating, and a paddle completed the standard specifications for the base model. Nowadays they are only used for tourists, but in days gone by they would have been used for fishing.

On the riverbank, right next to the coracle launch area, there was an enormous sign telling visitors, 'This area belongs to crocodiles'. There was a list of prohibited activities, including swimming, which we thought was very sensible. The sign informed visitors, 'Offenders will be punished' and to re-enforce the point there were two diagrams. One showed a police officer holding an offender in one hand and a big stick in the other hand. The other picture was of someone behind bars in prison. The message conveyed by the simple graphics was quite clear.

I asked Vikram if we should be worried about the crocs, and he said, 'Oh, it's not a problem now, sir, while the waters are low, they are only a problem when the water level is high and they can get near to people on the banks.' That was comforting to know.

Being old sea dogs, Nick and I boarded elegantly, narrowly avoiding the mistake of putting a foot through the bottom of the boat. We settled down, lying back against the sides of the craft, and were soon drifting very quietly downstream. As I drifted into a soporific slumber, I suddenly remembered another minor concern of mine. 'What about snakes?' I asked. 'Yes, sir, many snakes,' Vikram replied, and to prove the point he nodded towards one that was travelling through the water at high speed quite near to us. The snake's head, and the next 6 inches of his body (I don't know why I assumed it was male) were sticking out of the water like a periscope as he shot past, his tongue flicking in and out rapidly as he sped along.

As if to demonstrate how safe water sports on the Tungabhadra River can be, a couple of teenage Indian lads water-bombed their way into the dark flowing waters from the riverbank quite near to our flimsy craft. A very loud splash accompanied the sizeable ripple waves that radiated from their entry point and rocked our boat violently. Lads, eh? Perhaps they hadn't noticed the prominent signage with explicit graphics. I wondered whether it would be the snakes or crocs that got to them first.

Asha had one last stop for us. Anegundi Fort is a historical fortress believed to date back several centuries in one of the oldest inhabited places in the region. Positioned atop a rocky prominence overlooking the Tungabhadra River, the fort served as a strategic stronghold. We took a slow stroll up the hill to the fort and then beyond to the Durga Temple, dedicated to the Hindu goddess Durga. It was a bit rushed, in honesty, and felt a little like we were ticking the box again instead of dwelling on the significance of the fort and temple – but we did that later.

As we headed back towards Hospet at the end of our second gruelling day, Asha casually enquired whether we would like to see the temple where he was currently worshipping and sleeping overnight; we were quite close to it. Of course we did, so off we went. Asha asked us for some money first, to buy three packets of biscuits for the Baba's dogs and a bottle of milk for Baba. It turned out that Baba was the name of the holy man that lived at the temple. Asha had taken on the responsibility of providing the temple's two stray dogs with regular biscuit treats. After stopping for biscuits Asha headed his tuk-tuk to the hills.

A small concrete track led away from the main road, and slowly wound its way ever nearer to that famous location 'in the middle of nowhere'. Our tuk-tuk just about got up the steepest sections as the track wound ever higher. We had to get out and push on two occasions to stop the vehicle going backwards. Eventually, high in the hills, we arrived at the temple. More accurately, there were three tiny temples, each one very modest, small (only about 4 metres by 4 metres), and simple. They nestled between the rocks and boulders of the mountainside. One was painted white, another saffron, and another was covered in elaborate paintings of Hindu gods. The Om symbol seemed to be painted everywhere we looked, and there were several paintings of Ganesha. A small electronic plug-in device called 'Divine Voice' in one temple was broadcasting a repeating Om chant that provided a gentle background hum. Apart from that, there was silence. Two very slim dogs bounded up to Asha, tails wagging furiously. They clearly loved him, and they were possibly also enthused by the prospect of more biscuits.

Asha introduced us to Baba's son, a man of few words and a gentle smile who looked in his mid-thirties. He was dressed in a simple dhoti – a simple rectangular piece of unstitched cloth, wrapped around the waist and then tucked in securely. After being left to wander around the temples on our own, Nick and I were led up a few steps among the boulders to a rocky outcrop from where there was the most breathtaking view.

In front of us, across 180 degrees from horizon to horizon, was the magnificent vastness of the arid Hampi plain. The plateau was interrupted by a few scattered hillocks decorated with enormous blocks of sandy brown granite. Apart from the faint hum of the Divine Voice in the background, we stood in absolute silence. The light was fading, the day slipping away to join the shadows of the past. The sun was setting over a slightly Turneresque landscape painted in earthy shades of amber, apricot, and turmeric – Ganesha must have had some input into our arrival time. Thin wisps of smoke rose here and there, and we could just make out a few cars moving silently along distant roads. It was a jaw-dropping view and one of 'those moments'. Nick and I stopped in our tracks and tried to take it all in, both shaking our heads slowly in disbelief. I was almost afraid to breathe for fear of interrupting the moment. We felt so privileged to be in that spot, at that time, which seemed so achingly perfect. For me that was the moment of our trip – I'd have done the whole three weeks just for that moment and it still gives me goosebumps to think about it now.

Asha led us to a slightly ramshackle-looking building which turned out to be the home of Baba. We were invited inside to meet the great man, and his equally great wife, who immediately set about providing Nick and me with cups of warm sweet chai. A slightly surreal few minutes followed as we conversed with Baba's wife via our translator Asha, a cat wandered around the kitchen worktop, and Baba sat cross-legged on a mattress watching an Indian soap opera on his TV.

We left after twenty minutes feeling very privileged and very humble. Despite their simple lifestyle, our hosts were incredibly generous with their time and hospitality. Experiences like that make you question your values and re-evaluate what's important in life. As Asha drove us back down the mountainside towards our hotel Nick and I were left feeling so grateful for another very special Indian experience.

As we entered the outskirts of Hospet, the night sky seemed to crackle and flash, transformed into a dazzling spectacle by an uncoordinated pyrotechnic symphony. The first hint was a soft whoosh, followed by a burst of sparkling light… a shimmering star erupted and scattered high above. Then, another, and another, until the Hospet skies were ablaze with colours that painted the night.

We were back in the middle of the Diwali firework spectacular and it wasn't about to stop anytime soon.

Along the roadside, we began to notice the other ways in which homes, shops, and businesses were celebrating the Diwali festival of lights. Some were adorned with strings of colourful electric bulbs, creating dazzling displays that illuminated the surrounding buildings and the night sky – like Christmas lights back home… only with fewer reindeer. In contrast, other people opted for a more traditional approach, using diyas (clay oil lamps) and candles to illuminate their surroundings. Their flickering flames provided a sense of intimacy and nostalgia to the atmosphere, evoking the long traditions of Diwali celebrations. Driving past some houses, we caught glimpses of doorsteps adorned with intricate rangoli designs. They are traditional Indian art patterns created on the floor or ground using coloured powders, flower petals, rice flour, or other materials to welcome prosperity and good fortune. As we progressed further towards the centre of the town, we encountered more firecrackers and fireworks. Before long, we found ourselves driving through a cacophony of flashing lights and loud explosions. At one point, the traffic came to a complete halt as a series of detonations shook the road ahead and firecrackers lit up the night sky.

Back at the hotel, we stood outside for ten minutes, open-mouthed at the scale and ferocity of the ordinance going off all around us – like a combination of bonfire night back home and an army live ammunition training exercise. Our two full days in Hampi had been amazing, but there was little time to stop and reflect; the next day we were off to Mysuru.

CHAPTER 5

MYSURU – THE DAY AFTER THE NIGHT BEFORE

With Hampi filed away in the 'amazing… too much… must return' corner of the memory, we were heading next for Mysore, officially known as Mysuru. We had to take a relatively short hop of around 250 miles (about 400 kilometres) south into the state of Karnataka, but then we had two days in the place Mark Twain called 'one of the most beautiful cities in the world'. Though precise figures vary, Mysuru attracts somewhere between 8 and 10 million visitors annually, making it one of India's top-ten most visited cities. Although that can be put down to an attractive blend of history, culture, and vibrant attractions, its biggest draw is the magnificent Mysore Palace.

But first that short hop, which involved a car, a plane, and a train before we were delivered to our final destination by tuk-tuk. Heads still buzzing from the Hampi experience, we took a taxi to the unlikely tourist attraction of Vidyanagar and its airport.

The forty-minute drive eastwards from Hospet to Vidyanagar Airport, on the outskirts of the town of Toranagallu, takes you through a landscape that gradually transforms from quiet rural to heavy industrial. We drove on a surprisingly good road through arid countryside dotted with sparse vegetation and the occasional rural settlement. Our driver's idea of small talk was to tell us how good he is 'these days' with his alcohol consumption. His new-found discipline was such that he only hit the whisky one night a week. However, to make up for the rest of the week, his one night off the leash was a proper bender. Unfortunately for Nick and me, that was the night before our taxi ride. I'm not sure how he thought telling us that was a good idea, but we could tell the poor chap was still feeling hungover because he drove within the speed limit and on the left-hand side of the road nearly all the way to the airport.

Just over halfway to our destination we spotted two giant industrial chimneys on the horizon, their red-striped tops reaching high into the sky. As we approached the town of Toranagallu, the landscape became dominated by a sprawling expanse of industrial buildings that overshadowed all else. We didn't realise it at the time, but we were about to be driven through the sixth-largest single-location steel manufacturing facility in the world. We must have missed that when compiling our list of 'ten must-see tourist sites in India'.

Jindal Steel and Power Limited (JSPL) established its colossal Vidyanagar Steel Plant back in the 1960s, next to what was then just a village. The steelworks now cover an area of over 13,000 acres and has a production capacity of 12 million metric tonnes per annum, making it the largest single-location steel manufacturing unit in India.

As our hungover driver continued his personal journey back to the real world, he seemed to be operating on autopilot. He must have assumed we'd signed up for the add-on steelworks tour because we were soon being driven through an overwhelming industrial labyrinth of steel-clad buildings, pipelines, railway lines, conveyor belts, chimneys, and mysterious blocks of machinery decorated with twinkling lights. By the time we arrived at the airport, it felt like we'd driven around most of the 13,000 acres of the steelworks.

Nick and I knew nothing about this industrial tourist honeypot when we set off from Hospet, but this was India, and we'd have been disappointed if somewhere like that hadn't cropped up. This is one of the joys of travel, especially in India.

By choosing Vidyanagar Airport, we'd inadvertently stumbled upon an example of modern industrial India at close quarters. The largest steel plant in India was hugely impressive, and let's face it, it's not every day you get to see a steel plant with pair-cross technology, using pelletisation based on dry and wet process, and incorporating a twin-stand reversible cold-rolling mill. But those steel production technology ticked boxes aside, it's not the sort of place I'd want to hang around for too long… and Nick felt a long way from his Highland village. Despite its stark and borderline dystopian appearance, the sprawling steelworks was undoubtedly impressive, and a symbol of India's relentless pursuit of high-tech industrialisation. The country's remarkable economic growth is expected to make it the world's third-largest economy by 2030.

We wondered if we were in the right place when we arrived at the airport. We knew we were slightly early but there was almost no one around. The terminal building was very stylish, almost beautiful, with its sleek architectural design, clean lines and contemporary glass facades. But it was almost completely empty. It wouldn't have been the first time we'd found ourselves in the 'wrong' airport.

Once inside, we asked a couple of security guards where we could check in, simultaneously waving our flight booking form in their direction. With a smile and just a hint of head wobble, we were pointed towards some seating in a small, deserted waiting area in which the silence seemed to bounce off the glass walls. In due course someone dressed in airline uniform came through the front doors of the building and sat at what turned out to be the check-in desk.

An impressive mural inside the terminal depicts the history of the Jindal Vidyanagar Airport. Originally built as a private airstrip in 1997, it is owned by JSW Steel and sits on the edge of the giant steelworks we'd just driven through. Every giant steelworks needs its own airport. They have been handling commercial flights since 2006 as a bit of a side hustle... the company executives have to regularly go to Bengaluru anyway. At the time we were there, the airport had one domestic terminal, one runway, and one airline.

One of my guilty pleasures when travelling with my friend Nick is watching his regular 'discussions' with airport security staff. He has an uncanny knack of always being that person they pick out for extra checks. The nearest they've ever got to discovering his secret stash of firearms and narcotics was that time in Udaipur on our last trip to India, when they located his poorly concealed bag of Bombay Mix. In Vidyanagar though, it was his turn to watch, with barely disguised glee, as I was stopped to be searched. He collected his bag, stood waiting, and watched, smiling broadly at my inconvenience.

'Do you have a USB device?' asked the security man, nodding towards the x-ray machine.

'No, I don't,' I said, 'but I'm happy to open my bag to show you... Where do you think it is?'

'At the bottom,' he said.

'OK, I'll have to take everything out then,' I said.

He looked up and asked, 'Have you got an e-cigarette in there?'

'No, I've never even held one, let alone owned one,' I replied.

'OK then, take your bag – thank you.'

It was only when I'd retrieved my bag and walked through to the departure area that I realised my water bottle was still in my bag and full of water. I'd got away with that one.

We shared the flight with just a handful of other passengers. I remember two Dutch backpacker girls, an Asian mum with a dysfunctional toddler, and a couple of business executives, presumably travelling to Bengaluru on steel-related business.

I asked the female backpackers how they found travelling in India as women on their own because I'd heard mixed reports. 'No problems at all in three weeks – so far,' they said, which was good to hear. They thought it might not be so easy for Indian women. They'd heard plenty of stories about sexual harassment and violence but they wanted to believe things were changing. They mentioned things like the #MeToo movement which might be helping to raise awareness. One of them suggested 'they need more women in positions of power and more policies that promote gender equality… but from our experience as travellers, we've been fine.'

Apart from being an unusual airport, the flight was out of the ordinary for two reasons. First, it was a rare chance to fly in a turboprop aircraft, and second, our flight took off at least twenty minutes before the scheduled departure time. It meant we were landing in Bengaluru shortly after we were scheduled to leave Vidyanagar. You'll know by now these things just happen in India.

The second leg of our journey to Mysuru was a two-and-a-half-hour train ride, and for once we'd built in plenty of time to get from Bengaluru airport to the train station. Our taxi to the station took us down a very modern and busy six-lane highway and left us with more than enough time to find something to eat before we left.

Plenty of customers is usually a good indicator of a decent restaurant, so we dived into a crowded fast-food place near to the central railway station. For the equivalent of £1.60 for the two of us, we both enjoyed a delicious vegetable curry with coconut, a paratha, and a bottle of water. There was a high-intensity seating arrangement and we found ourselves sat with a couple of male students, dressed in trendy western-style clothes, complete with matching red Nike baseball caps. They immediately requested a selfie with us. It gave us an excuse to quiz them about their university courses and what they hoped to do when they qualified. They were both studying to be software engineers but one hoped to go on to teach. 'Education is the foundation for India's future,' he said, between bites of his crispy aloo tikki. 'The government has launched initiatives like "Skill India" to train youth in vocational skills and make them job ready. But the quality of education in our country needs improving at all levels, especially in the rural areas, like where we come from. The new National Education Policy is a step in the right direction, with its focus on holistic learning and flexibility. But implementation will be key... maybe we can be part of that.' That was the gist of his commentary anyway, from what I can remember. It seemed such a mature summary from someone who looked about twelve – but that's probably from my perspective, from which everyone looks a lot younger than they really are.

While we enjoyed the company, the food, and the great value, it did come at a price for Nick an hour or so later, which made him very grateful for his ample supplies of Imodium, but we won't dwell on that.

Our two-and-a-half-hour train journey passed very quickly, mainly because I was asleep for half of it. When I awoke, I found

Nick chatting to Hamis, a steel structural engineer (of course) going from Bengaluru to Mysuru for business. I found them deep in conversation about Indian politics. 'The upcoming 2024 general elections are going to be crucial for India,' Hamis was saying, as I looked outside and saw the countryside whizz by. 'The ruling BJP party has been focusing on issues like national security and economic growth, while the opposition is trying to build a united front. Caste and regional politics also play a significant role in shaping alliances. It's going to be interesting to see how things unfold and what it means for the country's future. I'm not sure about Russia… but at least it's cheap oil!' Despite only being half awake it struck me as an intriguing summary and I scratched around to find my pen and notebook to write it down as best as I could remember it. I could look at it later and ask Nick what they'd been talking about to try to make sense of it.

As if not wanting to be outdone by Air India, Indian Railways got us into Mysuru twenty minutes early. A short tuk-tuk ride to our guest house and we were settling down, shortly after midnight, to recharge the batteries ready for our first full day in Mysuru.

For breakfast, Nick and I headed to a place called Glen's Bakehouse, which we'd noticed the previous evening as we sped past in the tuk-tuk on the way to our guest house. The bakehouse appeared to be in yoga central, a district of the city with plenty of yoga studios and lots of people, mainly young women, wandering around with yoga mats tucked under their arms or slung over their shoulders. Set in pleasant grounds, the bakery was comfortable and clean and catered to both locals and tourists. As well as having a shop, there was a pleasant cafe which seemed to serve as a community meeting place.

We were lucky that someone came to help us with our order; they must have seen us floundering. The cafe had gone digital. Customers have to place their orders by using a QR code that leads to an online menu. We played the digitally inept pensioner card (which comes quite easily), and our helper eventually found a paper menu in one of the drawers behind the counter. The impressive range of items available included something called a Combo Breakfast, so when someone came to take our order I said, 'I'd like to choose some items from the Combo Breakfast list please.' I was told, 'No, sir, you cannot do that, you must choose the whole combo menu, you cannot choose separate items.' That was disappointing because I wasn't really that hungry, and it seemed wasteful to buy the whole thing and then leave most of it. There appeared to be no alternative, though. 'OK, I'll have the whole Combo Breakfast then,' I said. 'Certainly, sir, which items do you want?' The confusion might have been my doing, but I felt a bit happier when Nick's order of an Americano coffee with cold milk arrived as a milkshake.

Nick went over to the cake display to check out the real, analogue thing rather than the digital version. While he did so, I struck up a conversation with Rahul, a young software engineer who was sat at the next table. I told him we were trying our best but it's sometimes hard to keep up with technology. 'India has seen a massive digital transformation in recent years,' he said, sipping his chai. 'Everyone has smartphones and internet access now, people across the country are now connected like never before. It's changing the way we work, shop, and even access healthcare.' Rahul told me a little about the Indian Government's 'Digital India' initiative, but he recognised that progress wasn't something shared equally across society. 'There are still challenges, like ensuring digital literacy and bridging the urban-rural divide,' he said. I scrambled for my notebook again, thinking 'I'll never remember all this.' As a snapshot on India's progress in the digital world it was quite an eye-opener, and the QR code menu was tangible evidence of their direction of travel.

From the bakery it was only about 100 metres to the Badri Iyengar Yoga Centre, a place I'd previously identified online as somewhere we could drop into for a yoga class while we were in Mysuru. The familiar 'Iyengar' name made me think it might be somewhere where we could do something I'd recognise as yoga. When we found the building, it was locked up and there was no sign of life. It might have been closed for Diwali, like many places that day. I asked around and we were pointed to another studio a short distance up the road… the Nirvana Ashram. When we found it and enquired inside, we were told we should pop back in the morning to another building a couple of doors away – the Osho Glimpse. We walked up the road to make sure we knew where it was, so we wouldn't get lost in the morning.

On the way to the studio we got drawn into a game of street cricket with a couple of lads who looked about seven or eight years old. You know how it goes. Their kit list wasn't extensive – a short plank of old wood, whittled roughly at one end to form a handle, and a nearly-bald tennis ball. It was an even contest, the wily experience of two competition-hardened pensioners being offset by the vigour and athleticism of youth. I think I may have lost a yard or two of bowling pace over the years and the two lads didn't seem to have any problem spotting Nick's googlies. I blame the gnarled plank of wood, with a tennis-ball-sized hole along one edge, for my lack of runs on that difficult turning wicket. Having to move off the road twice, once to let a motor-scooter through, and then later for a passing goat, did nothing for my concentration as I tried to patiently build an innings into double figures.

Settling for (cough) an honourable draw, we went in search of a tuk-tuk to take us to Mysore Palace, which was top of our sightseeing list for the day. On the way there, expectations rising, I reminded Nick of the words of Lord Curzon, former Viceroy of India: 'Mysore is a jewel in the crown of India, adorned with a palace that surpasses many European wonders in its magnificence.'

We were indeed about to see something magnificent, but when we got there, we realised there were plenty of other visitors with the same idea. The queues were ridiculously long. We shouldn't have been surprised; the palace is the second busiest tourist site in India, and there were many Indian people on holiday because of Diwali. No problem. As soon as Nick had bought himself a sandalwood fan that he didn't need from one of the many persistent pavement hawkers, we decided to move smoothly onto Plan B. We'd work our way down our list of essential Mysuru tourist sites and then come back to the palace later in the day when the queues had died down.

Back to the tuk-tuk then, and off to the sandalwood oil factory. It was shut. No problem, off to the famous Mysore Silk Weaving Factory, then. That was also shut. Our driver then informed us that many places were closed for Diwali holidays. It was something that must have slipped his mind when he accepted our fares to take us to the sandalwood oil and silk factories. Ever helpful, however, and on the lookout for the next fare, he suggested we could visit the

Devaraja Market instead. 'It's a magnificent experience,' he told us, and available every day, including holidays.

Devaraja Market is a spectacle, like most Indian markets, but this one is particularly large and colourful. While markets have existed in Mysuru for centuries, Devaraja Market, in its current form, dates back to 1886. More than 1,000 shops and stalls employ over 3,000 people there, and with 8,000 to 10,000 visitors daily, it's one of India's busiest markets. A labyrinth of alleyways leads you past a mind-boggling array of stalls piled high with fruit and vegetables, flowers, spices, silk saris, incense, sandalwood products and essential oils. Fruit and veg might sound mundane, but the range of products is vast and here a stall of onions, for example, is more a vibrant art installation than a pile of root vegetables.

While primarily serving the local community, the market offers tourists like us an opportunity to glimpse a traditional element of Mysuru's daily life and culture. We found it relatively easy to walk around without too much harassment, although we were befriended at one point by a young lad offering his expert independent opinion while coincidentally guiding us towards his dad's essential oils stall. 'Only looking, sirs, just look.'

The market is a photographer's dream, with its vivacious colours and neat mountains of exotic products on a grand scale – you've never seen so many bananas in one place. Many stallholders craft elaborate flower garlands, while the stalls of kumkum, the powder used in Hindu religious and cultural practices, resemble an artist's palette with their vibrant cones of colour.

Nick and I have different recollections over how long it took me to buy a dress for my daughter Sarah. To me it was a snappy and efficient assessment of the options, but Nick's estimate of the time is given in hours rather than minutes. Anyway, after that, it was time for some late lunch, so Nick, who handles our nutritional well-being and social agenda, led us to somewhere he'd seen recommended. We escaped the hustle and bustle of downtown Mysuru for a couple of hours in the charming terrace garden restaurant of the Parklane Hotel. Labelled 'The Beer Garden' it was outdoors on the first floor, with terrace views, a constant distant symphony of car horns, and a very pleasant ambience. My takeaway memory from the place wasn't so much the good food or cool refreshing beers, it was the people we met. A group of six millennial lads sat near to us and were clearly enjoying a few beers and letting off a bit of steam. It was all good-natured stuff. I popped over to ask if they needed a professional photographer to capture all six of them in the same photo. That was the start of half an hour of playful chat and banter between them and two old Brits, with regular interruptions for photos. Their social media posts must have been buzzing. Eventually, we returned to our table to finish our beers and have a final chill before once again facing the fury of the Mysuru traffic and heat. When we came to pay our bill, we were told, 'No need to pay, those men over there have paid for you!' Despite our remonstrations our new-found friends insisted on paying for us – we were their guests in their country. More selfies, hugs, and extended hand-shaking. It was another example of the extreme generosity and hospitality we came across so many times in India – thank you again, lads.

It was too late to tour the interior of Mysore Palace, but we were told that if we timed our arrival for 7:00 pm, we would be there when they illuminated the building. The tuk-tuk driver who was driving us around that day thought it would be a good idea to see a genuine essential oils shop (i.e. one that belonged to a relative of his) and to kill some time we went along with his crazy idea. We arrived back at the Mysore Palace just as the lights went on – wow!

Over 100,000 light bulbs illuminate the grand building every evening for an hour. The times vary according to the day, time of year, and public holidays. It's a truly dazzling display that transforms the palace into a magical sight, showing off its enormity and its architectural grandeur. I saw it as a mixture of the British Houses of Parliament, Harrods, and Disneyland… but with Rajput-Mughal-Gothic influences, and all incredibly grand. We strolled around the grounds, looking in awe at the glowing palace, taking in the atmosphere, and being photographed by just about everyone. Dazzled by the exterior we couldn't wait to return the next day to look around inside.

The next morning, we were up early enough to arrive at the Osho Glimpse yoga studio at 6:30am. We met Valerie, a young Indian yoga teacher who was going to take us under her wing for the following hour. I have to hand it to Nick. He had tried yoga twice in his previous sixty-something years and decided it wasn't for him, but he was good enough to humour his old pal and put himself through a rigorous workout that neither of us really knew anything about.

Apart from Nick and me there were seven other participants in the class, four Iranian yoga students in their mid-twenties, and three other (also very young) Indian people. The studio was immaculate and well equipped. Over the following hour I recognised most of the postures we were led through, but it was the speed with which we moved from one to another that completely threw me. It was unrecognisable from anything I was used to back home in my beginners' class for oldies... It was like compressing four of my usual ninety-minute classes into one hour. Within minutes, we were gasping for breath, dripping in sweat, and slowly melting into our mats. I get the impression that young Indian and Iranian people cope with 30-degree heat and rapid-paced yoga in a confined studio slightly better than a couple of northern European white pensioners. Good God, Nick almost lives beyond the Arctic Circle.

Although Valerie was very sympathetic, and supplied suitable props at the appropriate moments, she took no prisoners when it came to the pace. The session ended with a relaxing five-minute wind down, lying down on the mat, flat on our backs in the savasana or corpse pose. By then, that's what Nick and I must have looked like anyway. It was a chance to completely unwind, made quite magical by Valerie's soft and gentle singing. After a few minutes, I wondered if I'd just died and was floating up to heaven accompanied by an angel's song.

We tried our best to stand upright and pretend we'd enjoyed ourselves. When we could breathe again, we got chatting to the other students. It turned out they were all on day sixteen of a twenty-seven-day intensive programme of yoga teacher training. Ha! Only day sixteen, they were lucky to keep up with us. We got a couple of selfies with Valerie and the other students and left the building, blinking in the harsh light of what was still early morning.

By the time we'd staggered our way up to Glen's Bakehouse for much-needed energy and liquids, we were almost out on our feet, slowly stumbling forwards in a state of existential vertigo. Nick managed to grab a chair and sit almost upright. As his eyes stopped spinning round, I asked him for his considered assessment of the yoga session. All he could mutter was, 'I don't think I've got control of any of my limbs at the moment.' I knew that was just his way of saying 'thanks, pal, I really enjoyed it.'

A fancy pastry something or other and shot of caffeine later and we were back in the land of the living again – time to head back to the palace then. The queues were much shorter this time. We bought our tickets at the South Gate, left our shoes in the designated racks and joined the procession of visitors working their way around the building.

Ranked second only to the Taj Mahal in visitor popularity in India, the palace was once home to the Wodeyar maharajas who ruled over the city from 1399 until India's independence in 1947. Built after the original structure was destroyed by fire in 1897, the current building, also known as the Amba Vilas Palace, was finished in 1912. Inside, we found a stunningly opulent and grand interior, with stained glass, mirrors, and colourful designs, along with intricate wooden doors, mosaic floors, and paintings from the Raj era. The sheer grandeur of the palace, with its intricate details and rich colours, from floor to ceiling, evokes the extravagance of an opulent time gone by. Designed by architect Henry Irwin, the palace cost 4.5 million rupees to build, which is almost £20 million in today's money. Back in the early twentieth century, it's hard to imagine the contrast between the palace's fabulously rich and exotic interior and the homes of ordinary Indian people.

The armoury, which holds over 700 weapons, was impressive, but the most memorable part of the palace for me was the Durbar Hall, a richly decorated balcony that served as a royal viewing gallery from which the maharaja used to address the public. You could just imagine the scene as the royal party and dignified guests

The Durbar Hall in the Amba Vilas Palace in Mysuru

sat in sumptuous luxury among intricately painted pink, yellow and turquoise columns, enjoying the glorious spectacle of marching bands and elephants during parades and festive celebrations.

We retrieved our shoes, bought some more water, and worked our way through the rest of our Mysuru highlights list. We returned to the silk factory to purchase some very expensive gifts for our wives (just in case they ever read this) and then headed for the shell museum and the sand museum. Both were interesting in their own ways, and worth the trip to see them, but the Mysore Palace is a hard act to follow.

The Guinness World Record Sea Shell Art Museum isn't just a tricky tongue twister, it's a private museum with a display of over 160 creations made entirely from seashells. I wouldn't call myself a great seashell art fan, but the chance to see a world-record-breaking sculpture – an 11-feet-tall statue of Lord Ganesha made with seashells and conches, is something that surely most people would find difficult to resist. You won't see one of those every day. Confusingly, the statues of Philomena Cathedral and the Taj Mahal are taller, but the record involves overall dimensions – this is India, so just go along with it.

The museum represents a labour of love by the artist Dr Radha Mallappa who should be praised for her great artistic skill and patient dedication. A short distance up the road from the shell museum is the Mysore Sand Sculpture Museum. There, you can explore over 150 amazing sculptures spread across 13,500 square feet, crafted from a whopping 115 truckloads of sand. Themes range from Mysuru's rich heritage and diverse wildlife to captivating stories from Indian mythology. If that becomes too exciting for you, it's possible to relax like Nick and I did, with a foot cleansing fish pedicure.

I will remember Mysuru as one of the most 'easy on the eye' of Indian cities. Wide streets and plenty of green open spaces were punctuated by grand white public buildings. Like Pune, Mysuru has garnered acclaim as one of India's cleanest cities, as recognised by regular government surveys. Our brief stay in Mysuru had been nothing if not varied. We'd experienced the body-wrecking joys of speed yoga, the cultural enrichment of the Mysore Palace and the boyish irresponsibility of a boozy lunch with the local lads. Our journey through southern India would next take us further south – to the largest bust in the world!

CHAPTER 6

THE LARGEST BUST IN THE WORLD

The label 'largest bust in the world' might attract visitors looking for something completely different, but what it refers to is a giant steel statue that stands 112 feet tall – the Adiyogi Shiva. The iconic statue rises from the foothills of the Velliangiri Mountains, at the Isha Foundation, near the town of Coimbatore, and is a symbol of inner peace and yoga's transformative power. It's a popular pilgrimage site in the state of Tamil Nadu, and a must-see for anyone seeking inspiration or with an interest in yoga and Indian culture. That was Nick and me. Once again, we had no idea what we were about to experience.

Back in Mysuru, our trip to Coimbatore got off to a stuttering start. It should have been a brief ride from our guest house back to Glen's Bakehouse for breakfast, but the first tuk-tuk we requested didn't turn up and the second one ran out of gas halfway there. Over breakfast, our team's transport liaison executive spent a long time on the phone trying to arrange our 150-mile trip to just outside Coimbatore, while I mainly drank coffee and praised his admirable perseverance and patience. Although Nick managed to make contact with several potential drivers on his Uber app, they kept disappearing before they got to us. Perhaps the distance had put them off, or maybe they'd found out who they'd be taking. Eventually one turned up, but he then insisted on charging double the fare he'd originally agreed. It was all to do with the difficulty of getting a return booking on a trip across two states, border taxes, meals, and a million and one other things... that I left Nick to negotiate his way around. He loves all that. Our eventual fare was the equivalent of about £30, which seemed reasonable for two of us, although it did mean rolling the dice on the Indian road survival game for at least another five hours. We bought some more water, threw our bags in the boot of the taxi and were off to Tamil Nadu.

Nick and I always seem to adopt the same seating arrangement in taxis. He sits in the front because he likes to be up with the action and is a natural conversationalist – he can chat away for hours about almost anything. Being more introverted, I'm perfectly content to spread out across the back seat, resting my dodgy left leg horizontally whenever possible. For some inexplicable reason, Nick decided to tap-dance on the landmine topic of Indian driving by bringing it up with our driver, Rahul. With typical male Indian driver bravado, he told us (as if we didn't already know) that 'anything goes' and if ever there are problems with the police, then 100 rupees will normally clear up any misunderstandings. To underscore his point, Rahul had his driver's rear-view mirror permanently tilted towards himself – not for seeing traffic behind him, but to check his hair. He further demonstrated his nonchalant attitude by unclipping his seat belt, prompting Nick to ask, 'No seat belt?' 'No need,' came the instant repost, 'no police here... I'm not a crash driver.' Well, that was certainly reassuring to hear, but then to bring that bold description into question he showed his signature move, which he repeated many times on the way to Coimbatore. When overtaking a vehicle, he would simply pull over to the opposite lane, staying in top gear, and then crawl past, no matter how long it took or how much the road changed during the overtaking procedure. His first attempt involved a bus, and we stayed out on the 'wrong' side of the road while we travelled about 300 yards, around blind bends and over the brow of a hill.

It feels to me like we all have a certain road mileage in India that we can expect to survive safely. Let's say it's about ten. The odds that your journey won't end well then shorten every marginal mile you travel after that. Whenever I step into a taxi in India, I think of Clint Eastwood playing the part of Dirty Harry and saying, 'You've got to ask yourself one question: "Do I feel lucky?" Well, do ya, punk?'

Before long we were out of the city and heading south into the pleasant Karnataka countryside. We drove for miles through a rural landscape that slowly unfolded to become very flat and almost featureless. Subtle variation was added by low, rolling hills, which emerged sporadically, eventually fading into the distant horizon. Occasional groups of emerald-green paddy fields brightened up the scene, and then tall clumps of deciduous woodland and plantations of teak and eucalyptus also did their best to break up the vast expanses of open rural plains. We passed through countless small, rural villages, each characterised by long rows of roadside buildings and dusty streets. Every settlement seemed to have lengthy terraces of single-storey flat-roofed shops set back either side of the road. From time to time we'd see a rendered wall painted with unusually bright colours, often yellow, displaying an equally brightly painted advert – usually for cement.

Goods of all types – mainly food or clothes, were everywhere out on display at the roadside, adorning the outside of the shops or on tables. In one village we drove through there were lines of tables displaying fish, marinated in something red and gloopy, and proving irresistible to swarms of flies. So many of the stalls were stocked high but we hardly ever saw anyone buying anything.

And so many billboards and advertising hoardings. There were always lots of scruffy motorbikes and scooters parked in rows alongside the main road, interspersed with cars, handcarts, rubbish, and stray dogs. While their wives got on with the hard work in the shops, thin leathery old men sat around on white plastic chairs chatting and watching the world go by, as they've probably done for day after day, year after year. The scene was the same in countless villages that we rumbled through, like a repeating piece of code in a computer video game.

About halfway through our journey to Coimbatore the open countryside became more wooded and in places we drove through dense forest. We drove through a series of large nature reserves before eventually arriving at the border with Tamil Nadu. Rahul parked up and disappeared into a green hut for five minutes, presumably to get his papers checked and pay taxes. When he came back, he wasn't happy. He told us how much he disliked Tamil Nadu – too many rules, too many taxes and worst of all, compulsory seat belts! He told us, with incredulity, the state was even talking about banning cigarettes. I liked the place already.

Once over the border, we were driving through the Sathyamangalam Tiger Reserve, one of the most important protected areas for tigers in India. It links the Eastern and the Western Ghats, creating a continuous habitat for the tigers and other wildlife. It was declared a tiger reserve in 2013, and according to the latest census, it's home to sixty-eight of the beauties, making it the fourth-largest tiger habitat in India. Nick and I didn't see any, of course, nor any of the leopards, sloth bears, wild dogs, hyenas, monkeys, or over 230 species of birds that are said to hang out in the reserve. We saw a deer though, much to Nick's amusement, because he sees them every day up in the Highlands of Scotland, usually feeding from the raised beds in his garden.

Rahul told us that the roads we were driving along were closed at night, for safety reasons, because that's when the wildlife comes out of the undergrowth to use them. When he used to work as an ambulance driver, Rahul would frequently have to gain special permission to drive through the reserves at night to reach patients. He regularly saw wild animals close up. We felt slightly cheated that we weren't seeing any of those amazing creatures. We got our hopes up when we saw a road sign for an elephant crossing, and plenty of elephant droppings, but Rahul told us confidently that we wouldn't see any. That seemed to do the trick. Within a couple of miles we saw two magnificent elephants close to the edge of the road and we got Rahul to drive slowly so we could get some photos. 'Be very quick,' said Rahul, 'It's a 5,000 rupee fine for anyone who stops their car.'

The forest grew denser, gradually transforming into lush jungle. Towering mahogany and teak trees clawed towards the sky, their leaves forming a high verdant canopy. Below, vibrant bougainvillea cascaded over glossy-leaved laurels and eucalyptus, adding a splash of colour to the luxuriant scene. Our route was taking us through the mountains of the Western Ghats and the eastern foothills of the Nilgiri Hills. We were entering the wild country and as if to reinforce the fact we saw a sign that read, 'Nilgiri Tree Forest – this land belongs to elephants'.

As we approached Dhimbam Ghat, where the road winds dramatically through twenty-seven hairpin bends down the mountainside, we briefly entered the UNESCO Nilgiri Biosphere Reserve. This vast reserve, spanning nearly 2,000 square miles across the Western Ghats and Nilgiri Hills, is a haven for a stunning diversity of wildlife. Over 5,000 species of flowering plants flourish across its diverse landscapes, while 550 species of birds, 30 species of reptiles and amphibians, 150 species of mammals, and 300 species of butterflies thrive within its rich ecosystems.

Splashes of red flag bunting adorned many of the villages we passed through after the reserve, a telltale sign of upcoming national elections. This triggered a passionate rant from Rahul about the BJP, their 'bad man' leader (Modi), and the rampant corruption in government. It all got a bit heated, with much thumping of the steering wheel. It's a shame we couldn't tease our driver off his political fence.

The hotel we were heading for was in the village of Alandurai, about 20 miles west of Coimbatore. On the map it looked like there was very little there, and when we arrived, we could see the map was right. We chose the hotel for its location and cleanliness, however, and on both counts it came good. It was clean and spacious and just a twenty-minute taxi ride from the Isha Foundation, and that big bust.

In hindsight, our research could have been more thorough. We knew we were going to see something recognised by the Guinness World Records as the 'Largest Bust Sculpture in the World', but we knew little more about it or the Isha Foundation.

The Adiyogi Shiva statue was inaugurated in February 2017, coinciding with the festival of Maha Shivratri, which honours the Hindu god Shiva. The name Adiyogi means 'first yogi' in Sanskrit, reflecting the belief that Shiva is the original teacher of yoga. The enormous grey sculpture, standing 112 feet tall, represents Shiva's head and is made from 500 tonnes of steel plates. The grand opening was a major event, attended by Indian Prime Minister Narendra Modi. His participation was seen as aligning with the BJP's focus on Hindu nationalism and potentially boosting his popularity. To mark the occasion, a book about Adiyogi was released, and a special song was composed.

The statue's height of 112 feet holds symbolic meaning, representing the 112 ways to achieve moksha (liberation from the cycle of birth and death) and the 112 energy pathways in the human body that affect physical, emotional, and spiritual well-being.

Founded in 1992 by Sadhguru Jaggi Vasudev, the Isha Foundation is a non-profit organisation dedicated to raising human consciousness. Sadhguru, regarded as one of India's most

The Adiyogi Shiva, Isha Foundation

influential spiritual leaders, envisioned the Adiyogi statue as a spiritual beacon. The Isha Foundation claims to have impacted over 200 million people worldwide, supported by 17 million volunteers across 300 centres globally. The 150-acre campus in Coimbatore serves as the global headquarters, housing the statue, a yoga centre, the Dhyanalinga (a meditative space), and various other facilities. Although their version of yoga, called Isha Yoga, is unique to the insights and teachings of its founding guru, it incorporates postures, chanting, breathing, and meditation common to many other forms of yoga.

The Indian national hockey team and life-term prisoners in Tamil Nadu jails are among those who have benefited from programmes conducted by the foundation. In addition to its focus on human well-being, the foundation runs projects aimed at planting trees and improving the planet's soils and rivers. Its educational initiatives are focused on providing underprivileged children with high-quality education. While the Isha Foundation is praised for its spiritual and environmental initiatives, it has also faced controversies related to land use, environmental impact, and certain aspects of its teachings and practices.

When we arrived at our hotel, in late afternoon, we enquired about the Adiyogi Shiva statue. We were given a leaflet by the receptionist and advised to head up to the Isha Foundation soon, to be there in time for sunset, shortly after which there would be a spectacular laser light show. That sounded a bit 'touristy' to us, not the stuff of hardened travellers – but it would be a shame to miss it. We didn't have much time, so we ordered a tuk-tuk and were soon on our way to see what a 112-foot-tall statue of Shiva's head looks like.

I think we were expecting a crowd of maybe a hundred visitors for the light show – maybe two hundred – but as we got nearer to the entrance to the Isha campus, the traffic began to build up significantly. There were plenty of tuk-tuks, taxis, private cars, and motorcycles, but most people seemed to be arriving in very noisy and colourful thirty-to-forty-seater buses. There was a steady stream of them, full of loud and excitable pilgrims. Many of the buses had elaborate paint jobs, loud sound systems, roof racks full of luggage, and even floral decorations.

Our tuk-tuk driver dropped us off at the entrance to the Isha Foundation and we began a fifteen-minute walk up a long drive. The stream of buses continued to roll past us, heading for the car park. The very impressive dark grey Adiyogi Shiva statue that soon appeared in the distance became even more impressive as we got closer and it was illuminated, as the light of the day began to fade. Before reaching the statue, we had to walk past an enormous car park, which was still filling up. We counted the long rows of coaches already parked and calculated there could be up to 10,000 people there. It wasn't what we were expecting. The throngs of people piling out of vehicles and heading for the statue were very enthusiastic, full of chatter and laughter, and very good natured. Apart from Nick and me, everyone seemed to be Indian, with quite a few dressed as monks.

In front of the eerie, imposing statue there was an open-sided temple and then a large, paved area on which people were gathering in couples and groups of various sizes. Despite the number of people, there was plenty of space; it never felt congested, overcrowded, or intimidating. Nick and I picked our way through to the front of the crowd and, like most people around us, we sat down cross-legged (until it became uncomfortable) on the warm, paved surface and took in the atmosphere. Away to our right, a rave was in full swing – a group of perhaps forty to fifty people were jumping up and down to very loud trance music that was being pumped out of someone's ghetto blaster. Everyone else was mostly chatting or staring up at the statue, which towered above us. Immediately next to us sat a group of twelve young millennial lads, dressed in nothing more than simple white dhotis or shorts. Before long we got chatting, and then there was the inevitable round of photos. They told us they were monks and were super-excited to be there. They also turned out to be a cricket team and they were visiting the foundation as part of a tour of the region.

The laser light show began on time, with the public address system booming out the story of Shiva and the origins of yoga in dramatic, echoing tones. It lasted for fourteen minutes and, as promised, was very impressive, with vivid colours lighting up the night sky. Afterwards, we joined the queue of people filing through the temple for a fire and water blessing. It seemed a good opportunity because I rarely get one of those back home in our sleepy Dorset village on a Tuesday evening – or any other evening for that matter.

After trying out my best sarvangasana and trikonasana yoga poses in front of the Adiyogi Shiva, we joined the thousands of others making their way towards the car parks and the exit. By now, the car park had also transformed into a mass catering venue. Rows of trestle tables had been set up and enormous pots of what looked like curry and rice were bubbling and steaming, ready for the return of the hungry pilgrims and coach passengers. We were told that some people come for the light show and then stay overnight for yoga and meditation the following day.

As we walked back to the site entrance, a constant stream of coaches filed past in a noisy and dusty convoy. When they saw a couple of odd-looking white men, many of the coach drivers felt compelled to demonstrate their vehicle's loud and impressive air-horns, prompting passengers to wave frantically, smile and shout out to us. It was all good-natured fun, and we usually responded with a loud and enthusiastic 'Jai Shri Ram!'

We got a lift back to the hotel eventually. Over a superb curry and a couple of Kingfisher beers, with World Cup cricket playing on the TV in the restaurant, we reflected on another amazing day. Sadhguru claims the Adiyogi is there to liberate us from disease, discomfort, and poverty – and above all, from the very cycle of life and death. While the jury is still out on that, our evening was certainly unlike anything we ever experience back home.

The laser light show had provided Nick and me with a memorable and unexpected experience. The following day we returned to the Isha Foundation to spend more time looking around, and possibly to find out what it was all about. I say 'possibly' because as I write this several months after our trip, I'm still not sure if I understand what was happening there.

Over breakfast we met a German woman staying at the hotel. She had come specifically to visit the Isha Foundation every day for a week. She was particularly enthusiastic about something called the Dhyanalinga. She explained that it was a meditation centre in which she spent several hours each day, and each time she emerged, she felt bursting with positive energy. We decided we'd have to give it a try later – if there's one thing I need most days, it's an infusion of positive energy.

We were dropped off at the Isha Foundation at a different entrance than the one we used the previous night. After passing through a reception area where we were invited to leave our shoes, phones, and cameras, we entered the grounds through security gateways. Visitors are guided along neat and tidy paths through beautiful gardens. The buildings, all architecturally elegant, are thoughtfully dispersed across the grounds, which are pleasantly filled with trees, bushes, and flowers. The large ornamental ponds, complete with beautiful lotus flowers, are surrounded by graceful palms. It is a beautiful place and must have cost a fortune, but at no point were we asked to pay anything to be there. There was an air of calm everywhere, and as we walked around, we came across many people on their own or in small groups performing yoga postures or meditating.

The paths lead visitors to two Theerthakunds. No, we had no idea what they were, either. Elegantly situated in vast underground spaces, they are like his-and-hers Olympic-sized swimming pools containing 'energised' water. The Suryakund is for use by men, whereas the Chandrakund, used by women, is said to be consecrated with more feminine energy.

It was all getting a bit too New Age and 'woo woo' for Nick, so he decided to skip the visit to the Suryakund and instead sat in the galleries high above the pool, writing in his diary and keeping an eye out for me. Already inclined towards New Age myself, I joined the queue of men heading for the pool and went into the changing area. You are given a small orange towel to cover your modesty and have to leave everything else in an unattended changing room. I reassured myself with the thought that people searching for spiritual well-being and inner growth probably wouldn't be the type to 'half-inch' passports and valuables.

Towel firmly in place, I walked down a set of stone steps and entered the pool. It is very grand, and impressive beyond description. Words can't quite capture it – you'll have to look it up online to see the images. The Suryakund is 20 feet below ground level, and suspended above the vast open space is a stunning 20-foot brass and copper sculpture of the sun. I watched the men ahead of me and followed their lead. It seems the thing to do, once you are in the pool, is to walk around the perimeter, stopping off at the midpoint of one of the longest sides so you can be immersed in a cascade of cool water entering the pool. You then walk up to three stone cobras that are coiled on top of columns near the centre line of the pool. The other men in the pool did lots of praying to the cobras, lots of full body immersions, and lots of cupping water over their heads. This isn't my normal daily routine but not to be left out, I did the same. This is supposed to sort out your pranic imbalances, enhance your physiological and psychological well-being, and heighten your spiritual receptivity. Prana is the life force or vital energy believed to animate all living beings.

Being a self-conscious soft lad from southern England this was all a bit out of my comfort zone, and while I was only too happy to give it a go, I'm not sure I was in the right mental state to fully benefit from a pranic reset or spiritual fine-tuning. For a few moments, however, it felt very calm and soothing. I certainly felt I was 'out there' experiencing something different, and that's one reason we go travelling. Trying to stay receptive to any positive energies that came my way, I got dressed and joined up with Nick again to resume our walk around the campus.

Near to the Theerthakunds, we stumbled upon the Linga Bhairavi Temple, described on one website as 'the ultimate manifestation of the Divine Feminine – powerful and all-encompassing'. Unlike most temples, this one is entirely managed by women, and many believe the temple has a powerful energy, particularly beneficial for women. Bhairavi isn't your typical gentle goddess. She symbolises strength and overcoming challenges. Some see her as a destroyer of negativity and ego, paving the way for spiritual growth. The good news is that the temple is open to everyone, regardless of religion or gender, so Nick and I channelled our female sides, which doesn't always come easy, and went in search of some spiritual energy.

Continuing our walk around, it wasn't long before we came across another 'world's biggest' – this time it was a 15-foot-high black bull called Nandi. He is the sacred bull whose role is to act as transport for the Hindu god Shiva. Nandi statues, typically a humped bull reclining on a raised platform, are often found outside temples dedicated to Shiva. Facing the entrance of the shrine, the positioning of the statue is significant, symbolising Nandi's unwavering gaze towards the deity he serves, waiting patiently to provide his master with his next ride.

As we walked past a large barn-like building, we were invited in for a free yoga session. Upon entering, we found ourselves alone. I sat patiently cross-legged staring at a blank video screen, while an Isha Foundation volunteer, dressed all in white, looked at her laptop and checked the door regularly to see if anyone else was going to turn up. Nick once again took a back seat and wrote up his diary. After a while, a group of about a dozen people had gathered. We watched a film in which Sadhguru talked about this vision of yoga and then a volunteer led us through forty minutes of very simple yoga positions branded as 'Upa yoga', or pre-yoga. The only bit I wasn't sure about was the rather long session of chanting at the end, but it was another fascinating experience and I'm glad I was able to take part.

If you think the Theerthakund pools sound unusual, the Dhyanalinga meditation space takes things to another level. In Sanskrit, 'Dhyana' means meditation, and 'linga' refers to form. The Dhyanalinga is essentially a giant sanctuary of stillness housed in a huge, dome-shaped building. There's no need to follow a specific religion or perform any fancy rituals; you simply queue up quietly for a while, and then enter. The atmosphere inside felt a bit like a church, but even calmer, if that's possible. The space was filled with people, mostly sitting cross-legged with their eyes closed in quiet contemplation. A few were lying prostrate and several had their hands clasped together in prayer. You walk around until you find a spot on the floor where you can sit. Then, just close your eyes, relax, and let your mind wander. At the centre of the dimly lit room, stands a large, smooth, grey cylinder on a plinth, illuminated from above to add to its dramatic presence. While the cylinder's role in relation to the Dhyanalinga's energy is open to interpretation, some people believe it helps channel or amplify the spiritual energy within the space.

It reminded me of the enigmatic monolith from the movie *2001: A Space Odyssey*. Just as the film's director left the meaning of the monolith open to interpretation, the purpose of the cylinder in the Dhyanalinga remains a mystery – at least to me. I suspect, much like the monolith, it alludes to themes of humanity's relationship with the divine, our place in the universe, and the nature of existence. Heavy stuff. Every ten minutes, a bell rings, and people get up to leave. But, you don't have to; you can stay as long as you like, and some people do – maybe for hours. The Dhyanalinga is said to possess a unique calming energy that invigorates everyone who enters, even if they have no previous experience of meditation and don't even know how to meditate. Imagine it as a quiet haven of peace with a giant battery that transfers positive energy and good vibes. That's the theory.

Nick and I left the building in silence, waiting until we were a respectful distance away before comparing notes. I reminded Nick that, according to Sadhguru, 'the Dhyanalinga manifests the exuberance of life in all its facets through the seven chakras'… and then asked him 'is that what you felt?' He gave me one of those knowing sideways looks and said, 'Not really.'

Me neither, sadly. If it was a doorway to enlightenment and spiritual liberation, it had remained tantalisingly ajar. I'm sorry to say neither of us felt anything unusual… apart from slightly stiff legs, and of course, the whole experience being very unusual. Perhaps it was because we were so far out of our comfort zones and not sufficiently relaxed to be receptive. It may be difficult to receive positive energy when your mind is racing and you're busy wondering what on earth you're doing there and whether everyone else is looking at you. I'm still open-minded, but Nick was more sceptical. We headed back to retrieve our shoes and phones and took one last look at the Adiyogi Shiva statue. With the rest of the day to get to our next stop in Munnar, we grabbed a taxi back to our hotel and packed our bags ready to move on once again.

Every tour of southern India should take in some tea plantations. Coimbatore lies roughly equidistant between two of the most famous tea-growing areas – the Nilgiri Hills to the north, which we'd passed through on our drive down from Mysuru, and Munnar to the south. Each is about three to four hours from Coimbatore by road, with limited transport options beyond taxis or buses. Visitors to Nilgiri can combine a tour of the tea plantations with a ride on the mountain railway, which takes visitors up to the famous hill station of Ooty. We, however, were heading further south, and after two hours of negotiating – assisted by the very helpful receptionist at our Sree Bharat Hotel – we finally secured a taxi to Munnar. We finally left at 3:00 pm, much later than we'd originally planned. We just hoped we would still get to Munnar at a reasonable hour.

Those hopes faded faster than a politician's promise when we met our driver, Santos. His English was limited, which is understandable since we were in India, but it was unusual for a taxi driver. He seemed barely old enough to drive, and his lack of experience was soon obvious. He drove very, very slowly, and often in the highest gear possible without stalling. He had absolutely no road positional sense and was very nervous of other vehicles, which is not typical for an Indian driver. After three excruciating hours we were only halfway to Munnar. Santos even stopped at the side of the road twice to answer his mobile phone. Every other Indian driver we'd met could juggle at least two phones, drink from a bottle of water, comb his hair, tune the radio, and still be able to hold a conversation with his passengers while breaking the speed limit and overtaking on a blind bend.

As the light began to fade, we entered the Anamalai Tiger Reserve, 370 square miles of protected area in the Western Ghats. We stopped at a checkpoint, where a barrier was raised for us, and then drove onto a single-track road with numerous speed bumps. Tigers and leopards roam the reserve, and as twilight turned to the dark of night, I recalled the words of Rahul, our previous driver, 'The tigers only come out onto the roads at night.'

Another hour into the journey, our patience was wearing thin. Santos's nervousness driving in the dark was apparent as he hugged the right edge of the road, where he could see it, only reacting to oncoming cars when they got close. Nick decided enough was enough and pleaded with Santos several times to let him take over the driving. I'm always the patient diplomatic one in these situations, but before long I too was pleading with Santos to let Nick take over the driving. I have known Nick's driving for five decades, so I knew what that meant, but desperation had set in.

We finally arrived in Munnar at 9:15 pm. By then, Santos's phone battery had died, so he had no way of navigating to our hotel. Fortunately, Nick's phone was charged, and he guided us safely to our destination. After being paid, Santos jumped back into his car and headed back to Coimbatore. It would be morning, at least, before the poor guy got back. Though relieved to have arrived, Nick and I were unaware that the stress of the day was far from over.

The photos on the online booking site for our hotel looked great. After the journey we'd just endured, we were looking forward to crashing out in our spacious family room with its panoramic balcony views over the town. However, we sensed something wasn't quite right as soon as we entered the hotel entrance hall. The guys behind the reception desk were flitting in and out of the building, flicking the pages of the room register backwards and forwards while occasionally glancing in our direction. We handed over our passports and the printed booking form. The man we assumed to be the manager then said, very sheepishly, 'Very sorry, sirs, there is a problem.'

When I asked what sort of problem, it turned out to be a 'no room' sort of problem. 'Very sorry, sirs, there is maintenance issue.' I asked what exactly they were maintaining, and we were told there was an issue with the toilet. But not to worry, according to him, because his brother had a hotel just down the road. Feeling we had no choice we followed the hotel manager a hundred yards down the road to his brother's hotel. It was dark and dirty. We were shown to a dingy room with a double bed, no towels or toiletries, and an overall sense of grubbiness. When we protested, we were offered another equally dark and dirty room, though this one had two beds. Eventually, a towel arrived, but it looked far from clean.

Nick and I are used to embracing the simple life with stoic nonchalance, when necessary, but the lack of Wi-Fi was a step too far! A sorry sign of the times perhaps, and maybe more our problem, but it disrupted our digital nomadic well-being. I'll not dwell on it because it was a rare negative experience, and we had very few of those in India. It was disappointing though, and after the journey we'd had, we both felt quite low. Still, you need the occasional experience like that to put all the other great ones into perspective.

CHAPTER 7

IT'S JUST YOUR CHAI TALKIN'

A full day in Munnar offered us the chance for a much-needed reset after the ordeal of our taxi ride from Coimbatore and the unforeseen hotel maintenance issues. With a whole day and a second night to enjoy in the 'Tea Capital of Kerala', Nick and I were determined to make the most of it.

Having learned the value of hiring a tuk-tuk for the day in places like Hampi and Mysuru we decided to follow the same winning formula in Munnar. That way we could use the driver's local knowledge to find us the best places… or the best places and the shop belonging to the taxi driver's cousin. First thing in the morning, we popped into the reception area of our original hotel to ask for a recommendation for a good tuk-tuk driver. As we entered, the manager was greeting an Indian family of five. The poor wife was trying to placate three tired and irritable young children and an emotionally troubled husband. Perhaps they'd just been dropped off by Santos after an overnight drive from Coimbatore. As I approached the reception desk, the manager's words were eerily familiar: 'I'm so sorry, but there is no room available now… there is a maintenance issue.'

Munnar, often called the Switzerland of India, cannot claim the clean efficiency or punctuality of its European counterpart, but the kitchen staff at our hotel clawed back some points with a hearty and enjoyable Indian breakfast. It might not have included pots of fondue or servings of hot raclette, but an omelette with coconut sauce, pickle, and idlis, with masala chai, was a pleasant surprise.

Munnar is a hill town that gets straight to the point: breathtaking scenery. Perched at 1,600 metres (5,249 feet) in the Western Ghats, it offers crisp mountain air and endless vistas of emerald tea plantations. Rows of tea bushes hug the rolling hills like a verdant quilt in India's largest tea growing region. Munnar isn't just about the cuppa, though. If we'd had the time, we would have explored the many hiking trails that snake through the hills, delving into the cool, green embrace of the dense forests.

The town itself is a charming mix of history and modern local life. There is a colonial-era Christ Church, with its stained-glass windows, and typical Indian markets overflowing with spices and textiles. Most of all, though, staying in Munnar is about soaking up some natural Kerala beauty and de-stressing from any travel and accommodation issues.

We had made a list of several places we wanted to visit, and when we found our tuk-tuk driver for the day, Mathan, he confirmed our list and even added a couple of extra locations. Off we went. We were heading for somewhere called 'Top Station'. The journey was about 40 kilometres, but we were assured there was plenty to see on the way. For any water infrastructure fans out there this will be right up your street – it's a two-dam trip. If you're also a fan of tea and succulent plants, your excitement will be off the scale.

As we left the town, it wasn't long before we were immersed in the rolling hills and tea plantations. Mathan explained the process for turning the landscape from its natural state into plantations. As he did so, the vista spread before us, laid out like a meticulously crafted demonstration piece for our enlightenment. Each element seemed purposefully arranged in order, as if awaiting our eager gaze to show us how the transformation takes place. First, the natural forest, predominantly consisting of teak and eucalyptus, is felled. In the second phase, everything is cleared away – trunks, branches, and roots are all removed, leaving a landscape of bare, rusty red earth. Access tracks are incorporated into the hillside, which is contoured if the slopes are very steep, and then the new tea trees are planted and staked. We must have seen examples of every stage of the planting process, from tiny bare twigs, through infancy to three-year-old bushes being picked for the first time. Those plants should then be producing tea leaves for another 100 years… that's a lot of cuppas.

Our tea production education just needed to be completed by a visit to a tea factory, and right on cue, we arrived at one: the Ripple

The hills above Munnar

Tea factory at Madupatty. The aroma of fermenting leaves hung heavy in the air as we made our way to the office to buy our tickets for the tour. Before going any further, let's briefly consider how India became the world's second-largest tea producer, after China. The country exports around 190 to 200 million kilograms of tea annually, with an export value of approximately $800 million. This is part of a multi-billion-dollar tea industry that plays a vital role in India's cultural heritage and daily life.

India's love affair with tea is a tale woven with threads of inspiration, discovery, and commercial opportunity. The delicate flavours of Chinese tea first enchanted British taste buds during the 18th century, but it meant a long sea voyage from China to Britain of around 16,000 to 18,000 miles (25,000 to 29,000 kilometres). The four to six months it took to complete that arduous journey by tea clipper was a long time to wait for your next cuppa. If only there was a part of the British Empire, closer to home, suitable for producing tea.

In the early 1820s, Robert Bruce, a Scottish botanist stationed in Assam, stumbled upon wild tea plants thriving in the region's damp and cool conditions. The discovery of these indigenous tea plants, along with a successful shipment of Indian tea to England in 1823, confirmed India's position as a viable tea producer. The British East India Company, always on the lookout for a profitable venture, then developed large-scale tea plantations in Assam during the 1830s and 1840s. Meanwhile, the story of tea was unfolding in another part of India – the misty mountains of Munnar. While Assam focused on the robust black teas, the high mountain slopes of Munnar provided ideal production conditions for an even wider range of tea types. The cool mists blanketing the hills, and rainfall well-distributed through the year, contribute to the slow growth of tea leaves, imbuing them with a delicate flavour.

In the late 18th and early 19th centuries, European explorers like the Duke of Wellington set foot in the hills around Munnar, and by the 1870s, activity in the region had surged. Pioneers like Henry Gribble Turner recognised Munnar's commercial possibilities, and in 1895, Sir John Muir acquired land concessions that paved the way for the formation of the Kanan Devan Hills Produce Company (KDHP) in 1900. With tea plantations firmly established, Munnar's economic fortunes blossomed, much like its tea bushes.

The 20th century witnessed rapid development in Munnar. Factories sprang up, transportation improved, and collaborations with companies like Tata Tea further propelled growth. During this period, the world's largest Instant Tea Factory outside the US, and Asia's largest Super Tea Factory were established. Munnar's tea journey, however, wasn't just about replicating success from other regions. In the latter half of the 20th century, the focus shifted towards innovation, with the introduction of organic tea cultivation and the creation of a fully automated tea factory. The 21st century ushered in a new era. In 2005, KDHP, a worker-owned cooperative, took over most of the tea plantations from Tata Tea, and that same year saw the inauguration of India's first Tea Museum.

From the early days of exploration and experimentation to the establishment of worker-owned cooperatives and a focus on unique tea varieties, Munnar has contributed several important chapters to the story of tea in India.

Nick and I were the only ones on the factory tour, a stroke of luck given the busloads of visitors that arrived later. Our guide, Ramesh, introduced himself and ushered us into the tea processing area. Ripple is the largest tea company in India, he told us, and there are sixteen factories in Munnar. Emphasising something that was clearly important to him, he told us that leaves are produced on a tree – not a plant or a bush.

As the rhythmic whirring of machines hummed a background lullaby, Ramesh explained that the factory processes a staggering 5,000 kilograms of fresh leaves daily, producing white, green, and black teas. The differences between these teas lie in how they are handled after being picked. We were shown boxes containing examples of the three main grades of tea: leaf, broken, and the rather unattractive-sounding 'dust'.

We made our way around the factory as Ramesh pointed out the various stages in the production process. When the harvested leaves (or 'plucked leaves', as Ramesh called them) first arrive at the factory, hot air is blown through them in a process known as withering. Next, machines macerate the leaves in a procedure called 'crush, tear, and curl'. The leaves are then rolled and fermented in large revolving drums to oxidise them. The fermented leaves are dried and sorted into various grades, ready for packing. In his inimitable way, Nick gave me a rueful smile and made a quip about our own withering over the years.

Ramesh threw a flurry of stats our way, and I scribbled them down as best I could while we followed in his wake. He wasn't hanging around. 'All the production stages are completed in just twenty-four hours… It takes 4 kilograms of fresh leaves to produce just 1 kilogram of black tea… The company's 12,000 employees are nearly all involved in picking the leaves, withering, and packing.'

At the end of the tour, Ramesh showed us out of the building, leaving us with a short walk to either the shop or the car park.

Nick pointed out to our guide, quite diplomatically I thought, the schoolboy error the company had made. The tour should end in the shop, where we would have felt uncomfortably obliged to buy some Ripple products. When the idea of providing visitors with a factory tour was first conceived, they must have thought it was just to inform visitors – missing the marketing opportunity that seems so obvious now. Sometimes, you have to think outside the tea bag.

By now, the area between the car park and the factory entrance was packed with a couple of coachloads of visitors. We'd been lucky to arrive when we did. We couldn't go without sampling a steaming cup of Ripple's best, however, so I queued up to get us a couple of cups of chai with ginger. When I say I queued up, it was just a free for all in front of the serving hatch. The crowd was three deep and more people were constantly arriving and jostling for position. I thought I was going to do my usual drinks-ordering trick of turning invisible, but perhaps being the only white person in the crowd and not aggressively thrusting rupees towards the tea servers and shouting at them worked in my favour. I took the two hot paper cups of chai back to Nick, who was by then sitting on a wall and sheltering in some shade from the strong late-morning sunshine. As he took a sip, I asked if he could appreciate the complex and nuanced flavours of tea and ginger competing for attention as they danced upon his tongue, testament to the expertise and care that went into the creation of the rich amber liquid. He gave me another one of those sideways looks and said a brief but meaningful 'yes'.

It was a short tuk-tuk ride from our mid-morning tea break to Carmelagiri Elephant Park. This was quite a shift in tone from the tea factory, but that rapid transition and contrast is something that is commonplace in India, especially with the crazy itinerary Nick and I had set ourselves. Earlier, we'd asked Mathan if there was any chance of seeing elephants on our way to Top Station. His response led us to this place, but the experience was disappointing.

The elephant in the room here is animal welfare. The four poor creatures we saw seemed old and tired. While they didn't appear to be distressed or mistreated, it felt wrong; those magnificent creatures should be out in the wild. Most of the visitors were families with young children, and the elephant park was a big hit with them. Scores of children queued up excitedly, waiting for a safari ride. Visitors were helped onto the elephants via boarding platforms. On top of each elephant was a large mattress-sized foam pad, and on top of that was a metal arched structure that supported a row of metal seats on either side of the elephant. The handlers led their elephants up a dirt track for 20–30 metres before turning around and coming back. We both felt uncomfortable being there, so we moved on.

As well as being ideal for growing tea, the hills around Munnar are perfect for the construction of dams. Next on our itinerary, still only 8 miles from Munnar, was Mattupetty Dam and lake, a popular tourist destination known for its scenic beauty and recreational activities. The area around the dam gets very busy during the most popular holiday times and weekends, and with our customary brilliant timing, we were visiting on a Saturday in the school holidays.

The Mattupetty Dam was built in the 1950s, when it was constructed by the Kerala State Electricity Board for hydroelectric power generation and irrigation. Built across the Kundala River, a tributary of the Periyar River, it stands at a height of 83.35 metres (273.5 feet) with a length of 238 metres (780 feet). The reservoir created by the dam has a storage capacity of 55.4 million cubic metres and covers an area of approximately 13 square kilometres (5 square miles). That's a lot of stats and a lot of water… think of it as similar in size to Thirlmere, in the Lake District National Park in Cumbria. One of the lake's many uses is for boat rides, which offer stunning views of the surrounding hills and forests. We took a few photos of the dam and wandered among the multitude of souvenir and food stalls. We were tempted to try some street food – which in India can be either incredibly adventurous and rewarding or downright bloody stupid. The deep-fried chillies would have been an intestinal risk too far, so we opted instead for some alarmingly bright yellow deep-fried bananas. They were fantastic… although Nick had reason to disagree with that assessment later in the day. The place was buzzing with visitors, so we decided to move on again towards Top Station.

The twisty narrow road followed the southern shore of the reservoir eastwards, towards towering mountaintops. As soon as Mathan told us we were heading for a lakeside tourist spot called 'Echo Point', the jukebox in my mind flipped back to select a 1980s classic. Our next stop was only 4 miles down the road, but I'd already told myself it was far away in time. It's lucky we weren't there to see the sun go down or the song would be stuck in my head all day.

Echo Point is a popular tourist destination near to where the stunning mountain ranges of Mudrapuzha, Nallathanni, and Kundala converge. This unique spot is renowned not only for its natural echo phenomenon but also for its breathtaking views, as the three mountain ranges frame the serene landscape, creating an ideal backdrop for visitors seeking both tranquillity and adventure.

Nick and I bundled out of the tuk-tuk when we arrived, and looked down at the shimmering green lake from the roadside. The other side of a metal fence, supporting a sign saying 'Gov of Kerala – Prohibited Places', was a crowd of around a hundred people. Most were standing around admiring the panoramic views of the surrounding hills and forests. Some were yelling at the tops of their voices to get that echo, some were taking selfies (obviously), and some were queuing up for rides in pedal boats. They were an addition that somewhat marred the natural beauty of the place, but we couldn't complain – we were adding to the tourist numbers ourselves. And if there's a rupee to be made…

Our ride to Top Station, located on the border between Kerala and Tamil Nadu, continued along even more narrow twisty roads that were getting slowly more congested as the day wore on. As we ascended higher, through plantations and forest, we began driving in and out of wispy clouds, and the atmosphere became cool and damp. Twenty miles from Munnar, we finally arrived at our destination, where our driver found a parking spot among a throng of coaches, taxis, private cars, and tuk-tuks.

Situated at an altitude of around 1,700 metres (5,577 feet) above sea level, Top Station is the highest point on the Munnar-Kodaikanal road through the Western Ghats. It offers breathtaking views of the surrounding landscape. A panoramic vista of rolling hills, lush green valleys, and tea plantations stretches as far as the eye can see. The vast expanse of the Theni district in Tamil Nadu, with its winding roads, small villages, and patches of dense forests is backed by the impressive Meghamalai mountain range. The view is spectacular – though Nick and I had to take the guidebook's word for that, because we saw none of it; for the last twenty minutes of our journey to Top Station we drove through thick clouds.

From where Mathan dropped us off we walked through a long temporary village of traders' stalls out to the 'viewpoint'. There was a concrete platform from which, on a clearer day, there would have been a steady stream of 'oohs' and 'aahs' from satisfied visitors. But for us, the mist hung in the air like a heavy white curtain. We bought some delicious fresh-boiled corn on the cob from one stall – it felt like the steam was adding to the foggy atmosphere. Nick also picked up a very fetching woollen balaclava helmet – not an obvious clothing choice for India, but he assured me it would be put to good use when out on the mountains of Scotland. Most of the food stallholders had pet dogs and we quickly saw why. A group of monkeys regularly descended from the surrounding trees to raid for food. The dogs, fully aware of their responsibilities, barked enthusiastically at the monkeys to scare them away whenever they appeared. Some very clever monkeys seemed to be working in teams, using diversionary strategies. It was an amusing sideshow, but we'd have preferred the view. C'est la vie. We began the long drive back to Munnar with a couple of more stops planned for the way back.

We stopped for half an hour at the Kundala Dam, constructed in 1946 primarily for irrigation and to support the local tea plantations. The dam is relatively small compared to the Mattupetty Dam, with a height of about 46.93 metres (154 feet) and a length of 259.38 metres (851 feet). Notably, for all dam enthusiasts reading, Kundala Dam holds the distinction of being Asia's first arch dam. We didn't see it, but the nearby Kundala Golf Course is one of the highest golf courses in the world, situated at an altitude of approximately

6,000 feet above sea level. While I admired the beautiful lakeside scenery, Nick invested 5 rupees of his hard-earned pension on an increasingly urgent visit to a public toilet. He dashed off in a bit of a hurry muttering something uncomplimentary about banana fritters.

In India, public toilets are limited, especially in rural areas, despite government efforts like the 'Swachh Bharat Abhiyan' to increase availability. Travellers should rely on facilities in hotels, restaurants, and malls, and carry essentials like tissues, hand sanitiser, and coins for pay-to-use toilets. There were ladies and gents toilets at the dam, and both had long lines of women standing outside. For some reason the ladies thought it was very amusing when Nick joined them, although, thankfully they didn't go as far as asking for a selfie. Nick came back very relieved; it was 5 rupees very well spent.

Our last stop, before returning to Munnar, was at the Carmelgiri Botanical Garden, which was established in 1992. Its current sign shows that it has broadened its original scope to become a 'Tea, Spices and Chocolate Park'. I imagine that's quite a niche sector. The gardens cover an area of 5 acres, hosting a collection of over 300 species of plants, both native and exotic. The gardens are divided into different sections, each showcasing a unique collection of flora. Cacti are a speciality, and if you're a fan, this is definitely the place to visit. Towering palm trees announce the exotic plants section, which also includes giant ferns and striking orchids from various parts of the world. The colours were so vivid and the shapes so unusual that it sometimes felt a little unworldly.

One of the most interesting sections was the one dedicated to medicinal plants, which contained herbs and shrubs known for their therapeutic properties. The garden boasted a collection of over 100 medicinal plant species, many of which are used in the ancient Indian system of Ayurveda. Ayurvedic medicine relies heavily on the use of herbs and plants to promote balance and well-being in the body. I'll come back to that in the next chapter when Nick and I visit a specialist Ayurvedic garden. We didn't spend long in the gardens, but it was an interesting and worthwhile stop – it's not every day you get the chance to see one of the largest collections of cacti in southern India. It was an enjoyable and educational experience, capped by meeting a lovely group of female Indian teachers just as we were about to leave. Not so fast – time for at least a dozen photos.

It had been another busy day. We wound our way back to Munnar through the tea plantations, stopping several times to take photos. The scenery might have been largely influenced by man, but it was still beautiful. Up in the hills around Munnar you leave behind the familiar high-level haze that you experience in many parts of India; the air is clean and fresh. The emerald-green rolling terraces of tea bushes/plants/trees looked dazzling in the clear mountain air, under bright blue skies, with a mountainous backdrop and occasional wispy streaks of cloud. Inspired by the scenery at one of our photo stops I struck up a yoga 'Tree Pose' (Vrksasana). Somehow it seemed the right time and place… and anyway I'd promised to send the occasional yoga photo to my teacher back home.

Back in Munnar, we went back to our original hotel, where we had been promised a room for our second night. There was one, but it lacked the advertised amenities – no shower, no bath, no toiletries, no Wi-Fi, and no balcony with views over Munnar. We discussed the situation with the manager, using as exhibit A, the printed room description and photo. The result was a discount. It was all quite civilised, and it was time to put it all behind us.

Fulfilling his catering and hospitality responsibilities admirably, Nick had found us another great restaurant for our evening meal. 'The Residency' lived up to expectations and came with an unexpected entertainment package. We'd just taken our seats when an English guy came over, and as he pulled out a chair at our table and sat down, he asked, 'Alright if I join you lads...? Just say if it's not.'

I'm going to call him 'David', and he was quite a character. Very sensibly, he was spending the six cold months of the year living in India and then going back to Blighty for the summer. David was clearly in a committed relationship with Kingfisher beer and had already sampled one or two before he joined us. In his introductory remarks he announced he was studying for a PhD in analytical psychology and his thesis was something to do with 'finding a hidden god'. At least that's what I remember from the evening – it might not be 100 per cent accurate. He quickly followed up by declaring, 'I have skin in the game', which turned out to mean he was a practising Catholic. I complimented him for including India in his search for God but questioned whether he was really looking for a god or merely trying to justify the one he already had. That got a robust response and took the discussion down a side street onto a brief theological mystery tour.

As the evening wore on (the meal was superb, by the way) and the beers flowed, the discussion became even more philosophical. David's language became more colourful and base. He wasn't averse to the occasional outburst of insults to either Nick, or me, often using anatomically graphic language laced with robust Anglo-Saxon adjectives. As bad as that sounds, he somehow delivered his filthy abuse with good humour. I loved our discussion and what I really appreciated was how we could question anything that David said and provide counter-evidence to his points of view, and he took it all in good humour. Well, apart from those outbursts of filthy expletives. Good lad. We had an amusing and intellectually stimulating discussion. We went our separate ways just as we were all beginning to talk a common language – fluent slur.

Nick and I reflected on another interesting day and a thought-provoking night out as we walked back to our 'luxury' room. We only had two nights in Munnar, but it had been well worth including on our itinerary. The next day we were heading back to the coast, to Kochi.

CHAPTER 8

THE QUEEN OF THE ARABIAN SEA

For a couple of self-confessed Indian Railways superfans, Nick and I seemed to be doing a lot of travelling by car. There were life expectancy and blood pressure issues associated with that strategy, but on the positive side, it was a good way to see the country close up. On a practical level, for the route we'd chosen through southern India it was often the *only* travel option. It's the Western Ghats – they get in the way.

The distance between Munnar and our next port of call, Kochi (also known as Cochi, or Cochin), is approximately 130 kilometres (81 miles) by road, east to west. However, because of the winding and hilly nature of the route, it typically takes around four to five hours to drive, depending on traffic conditions, vehicle, and driver. That's unless you are driven by our friend Santos from Coimbatore, in which case it would be nearer four to five days.

Whatever was left of the day when we arrived in Kochi would be all the time we had to explore and enjoy the place. I'm ashamed to admit how little time we'd built into our schedule (again), and I should take full blame for that. Nick had craftily left that side of things to me. It was yet another place where we didn't really have enough time to do it justice. It would be another box ticked, but as usual, we were excited to explore somewhere new, and having done our homework, we could still squeeze a lot into our flying visit.

Back in Munnar, we waited with eager anticipation to meet the taxi driver who was going to take us to Kochi for the next leg of our adventure. Pranav arrived at our hotel in a sporty blue Daihatsu. It was very impressive. Blue fur covered the seats and dashboard, and there was a matching blue glass (plastic) gear stick. The car had an upholstered interior roof and a seriously pimped-up entertainment system. I was just waiting for our driver to say, 'You've never heard of the Pranav Falcon? It's the taxi that made the Kochi run in less than twelve parsecs.'

I was impressed, but also wary. Even more so when I spotted the black feather dream catcher dangling from the rear-view mirror. What was all that about? Was it a sign we needed spiritual assistance to survive the nightmares of the road ahead?

It was going to be interesting; most taxi drivers we'd met were scary enough in slow cars. I just hoped I'd have reason to fill in a few more chapters of my gratitude journal by the end of the ride. We bundled our luggage into the boot and took up our usual seating positions; Nick next to our driver and me in the back. Positioned in the centre of the rear seat I was well placed to fully appreciate Pranav's acoustically augmented sound system. The two huge speakers on the rear shelf, with enhanced bass, wouldn't have been out of place on the Pyramid stage at Glastonbury. Feeling cool in my shades, I tapped my foot to Pranav's choice of Desi Beats tracks as we drove through the outskirts of Munnar. We were treating anyone within 50 metres of the road to a free concert and who doesn't enjoy a bit of Panjabi MC on maximum volume?!

Well, I didn't after a while. As good as it was, it began to dawn on me that another four and a half hours of the same thing might leave me with permanent hearing loss. About then, my head began to throb with each beat, and I could barely hear Nick when he tried to talk to me. I tapped Pranav on the shoulder and asked if he wouldn't mind, please, turning the music down a little. So British; I felt I was apologising. Nick stepped in with a brilliant diversionary tactic, asking Pranav if we could listen to commentary from the World Cup cricket final that was just about to start. 'No problem.' In fact, Pranav could do much better. In the centre of his dashboard was an in-car entertainment screen and after about fifteen minutes of searching, while only partially observing the twisty mountain roads and undertaking multiple risky overtaking moves at high speed, he found us live TV coverage! Fortunately for us, Pranav was an excellent driver. Even with his attention diverted from the road for most of the fifteen minutes he was scrolling the screen, he drove no worse than any other taxi driver, and considerably faster. I don't know how he did it, but somehow he did.

The journey from Munnar to Kochi is scenic, passing through lush green hills, tea plantations, and picturesque towns like Adimali and Kothamangalam. The route also includes a few hairpin bends and steep inclines. Pranav saw these as a challenge; could he maintain the same progress without dropping speed?

Before we left Munnar, we'd asked him if there were any scenic places where we could stop on the way, and he had two in mind for us. We had the briefest chai stop at the Kallar Falls, but a longer break at the Kerala Spice Farm, one of many in the area. Kerala's fertile soil, warm climate, and ample rainfall create the perfect conditions for growing a wide variety of spices, which has helped to make the state a global leader in spice production. For centuries, Kerala's spices have attracted traders from around the world, shaping the region's history and culture.

Pranav parked his car outside the Spice Farm shop and went in search of some chai while his car engine and tyres cooled down. He looked confident that his choice of soft compound tyres and a two-stop strategy would result in a new speed record by the time we reached the finishing line in Kochi.

Nick and I went to look around the farm. We soon found ourselves hooked up with a guide, Amal, and being driven down a steep hill in a jeep. It was only a short distance to the farm display area, where Amal led us, tree by tree, bush by bush, around the grounds, stopping to tell us about each plant and how it could help to prevent or cure various ailments. He scampered up trees with remarkable agility, plucking off samples for us to taste. 'Try this one,' he said, opening up and handing us a couple of fruits that looked like mangos or small melons. Following his lead we tasted some of the white, fleshy pulp inside. Its complex flavour blended sweetness and tartness with hints of citrus or tropical fruits. It was delicious – and turned out to be the edible part of a cocoa fruit. The large, rich brown seeds in the centre, the cocoa beans, require processing before they can become chocolate.

Amal certainly knew his stuff, and his enthusiasm, despite how many times he must do the same circuit each day, seemed genuine. He was a big fan of Ayurveda, a subject that Nick and I knew little about. It's a 5,000-year-old system of traditional medicine that emphasises the balance of mind, body, and spirit and is deeply ingrained in Kerala's culture. With numerous Ayurvedic hospitals, clinics, and resorts, Kerala has become a hub for wellness tourism, attracting visitors from around the globe.

Unlike the tea factory, the Spice Farm had recognised the marketing advantage of ending their tours in the shop. When we were asked if there were any Ayurvedic treatments or essential oils we were interested in, I made the mistake of saying I knew little about them. We were invited to sit down, and we received a combined lecture and hard sales pitch from a beautiful young woman with eyes that sparkled and a captivating smile that could have featured in a toothpaste advert. She possessed a certain... aesthetic appeal, that would disarm even the most resolute bargain-hunter. That was tough. I think Nick was more resilient, but she had me wrapped around her finger until she got to the purchasing recommendations. She explained how there were two basic categories of Ayurvedic medicine. One to treat problems of the mind and one for body ailments. She confidently prescribed a two-month cure-all. If I understood her correctly (I almost certainly didn't), these remedies could fix anything. Thinking of one or two long-standing issues I have, such a claim seemed improbable. Maybe the prescribed medicines were more preventative, for people starting with an already well-functioning mind and body. Anyway, the spell had been broken and Nick and I shuffled out of the shop without buying anything. I'm probably overcautious when I travel, but my default position is to always be cautious. I've regretted that many times, when met with incredible kindness, but I've also had many occasions when my caution has been justified.

Still wondering if we'd had a lucky escape or foolishly missed out on the opportunity of purchasing a lifetime cure for everything, we met up with Pranav and continued our journey westwards. Our last stop on the road to Kochi was at a small restaurant in a village about 35 miles from our destination. The dal makhani with egg masala we had there was very simple, but beautifully tasty. The aroma hit us first as it was brought to our table, a wave of warm spices – cumin, coriander, and a hint of smokiness. Deep black lentils were sprinkled with bright orange tomato and creamy swirls of butter. It was a treat from the first bite, one of the meals of our trip, served up by the cheerful owner for very little money in a modest roadside cafe.

Once back in the car, Pranav was soon going through the gears to push his car into hyper-drive for the final few miles of our journey.

Kochi, known as 'The Queen of the Arabian Sea', is a busy port city with a rich history and a unique blend of cultures. It has been a hub of trade and commerce for centuries, attracting traders and explorers from around the world. This influx of foreign influence is evident in the city's architecture, cuisine, and way of life, making it a fascinating destination for tourists, of which there are many. Kochi's strategic location on the Arabian Sea, coupled with its well-equipped port, has made it an increasingly popular stopover for cruise ships.

The city has no shortage of historical sites to captivate visitors and their cameras. The Santa Cruz Cathedral, the Jewish Synagogue, and the iconic Chinese fishing nets that grace the coastline and feature prominently in every tourist's photo album are just a few examples of the city's rich heritage. That's quite a list, especially for two fellas only stopping for one night.

Pranav stopped his car where our accommodation for the night should have been. We were on a small promontory, very near to the Kochi seafront and close to the famous Chinese fishing nets and the Kerala Kathakali Centre. Good planning for later, I thought, but maybe not if we didn't have anywhere to stay. There was nothing there resembling the address we had been given. I phoned the owner and they confirmed we were at the right drop-off point, so we said our farewells to Pranav and he disappeared in a cloud of dust and burning rubber.

What followed was strange, but we were in India, so perhaps not. As we stood at the roadside, an elderly woman (i.e. about our age) appeared. Her English was about as good as our Malayalam, the local language, so there were few words spoken but lots of hand gestures and pointing at maps and booking forms. She led us the short distance to her house where we were invited in and asked to sit down. After ten minutes of awkward non-conversation, a young lad appeared outside on a motor-scooter. He asked us to follow him. Perhaps identifying me as the more weary-looking pensioner, he put my rucksack in the footwell of his scooter and Nick and I walked behind in his wake to the next road. We'd finally arrived at our accommodation for the night, and we were warmly greeted with iced lime drinks.

It was already late afternoon, and there wasn't much time left for sightseeing. We unpacked, showered, and set off to see what we could find. The Kerala Kathakali Centre was close by, and we soon had tickets for the evening show in our hands. Another twenty-minute walk through the Fort Kochi area and we were stood on the seafront by the famous Chinese fishing nets. Known locally as 'Cheena Vala', the iconic structures are massive cantilevered fishing nets that have been in use for centuries. Chinese explorer Zheng is believed to have introduced them when he dropped in during his travels in the 15th century. The nets are held in teak wood frames and bamboo poles, which extend up to 10 metres horizontally over the water, counterbalanced by large stones tied to ropes on the other end, allowing the fishermen to lower and raise them with ease.

The Chinese Fishing Nets, Kochi

The number of tourists we were seeing and hearing had increased significantly in Kochi and for the first time on our trip we were coming across plenty of Europeans and Americans, as well as Indian tourists. Nick and I felt quite put out by how many foreign tourists there were… We thought we had India to ourselves. There must have been a cruise ship visiting.

After witnessing the iconic Chinese fishing nets, we made our way to the Kerala Kathakali Centre for the evening performance. It was a modestly sized theatre but that made it feel more intimate.

Three performers were on the stage as we took our seats: two sitting and one lying down. Meticulously applying layers of vibrant paints and powders to their own and each other's faces, they slowly morphed into the larger-than-life characters of the Kathakali tradition.

Kathakali, a classical Indian dance drama, originated in Kerala during the 17th century. It combines dance, music, and acting to tell stories from Hindu mythology, particularly the epics of Mahabharata and Ramayana. The performances are known for their elaborate costumes, intricate make-up, and stylised gestures, which convey a range of emotions and actions.

It was a diverse audience of locals and tourists, but I think the majority must have been on a cruise liner stopover. One performer gave an explanation and demonstration of the art of Kathakali prior to the performance, so the audience could understand what the make-up represents, what the different mudras mean and what the plot of the story was. Mudras are the stylised hand gestures and finger positions used by the performers to convey specific meanings, emotions, and actions. The twenty-four basic mudras in Kathakali each have their own specific meaning but can be combined and changed to create a vast vocabulary of gestures that can convey everything from simple actions like walking, eating, or sleeping, to more abstract concepts like love, anger, or despair. The way the performers contorted and controlled their facial muscles, in particular, was mind-boggling, and must have taken years of dedication and practice.

The story unfolded through a series of scenes, depicting the eternal struggle between good and evil. The performers' expressions were exaggerated, making it easy for the audience to understand the emotions and intentions of each character. A live musical accompaniment, featuring traditional instruments like the elathalam (a pair of small, thick cymbals), chenda and maddalam (types of drum), added to the intensity and drama of the performance. It was a very simple story, and I hope this isn't too much of a spoiler for anyone going to see the play if I tell you the bad guy wanted to take the good guy's woman, nearly succeeded but then got his comeuppance.

The message of the triumph of good over evil resonated with the audience. The bad guy got what he deserved, we all clapped furiously in a standing ovation, and all was well with the world. After the performance, the audience was invited to join the performers on stage for photographs. Most people left, perhaps they had a boat to catch, and a few new people came in. At this point Nick had a minor panic attack when he realised he had no beer for later in the evening. There was a brief interlude before the martial arts demonstration began, so Nick left me mixing with the actors on stage while he dashed off in search of an English wine shop.

The term English wine shop is confusing when you first come across it. Don't expect to find a tweed-clad proprietor waxing poetic about the virtues of English viticulture. In India, an English wine shop is simply a colloquial term for an off-license, or a liquor store, as it's known in the US. They sell a variety of alcoholic beverages, including beer, spirits – and sometimes even wine – for customers to purchase and consume off the premises. The term is a remnant of the British colonial era, when such establishments were introduced to cater to the British population in India. They can be found in most cities and towns across India, and everyone seems to know where you can find one. Ranging from small, ramshackle hole-in-the-wall establishments to plush modern stores, most are the former.

Half a dozen people from the audience, including me, went on stage to meet the actors and, of course, get a few photos. Despite their fairly scary make-up, the artists were very warm and welcoming, happy to share a photo and to share their passion for their ancient art form.

Nick returned, mission accomplished, halfway through the demonstration of Kalaripayattu, the ancient martial art form of Kerala. The young lads on stage displayed incredible agility, strength, and control as they performed various combat techniques and acrobatic moves. It was a mixture of gymnastics, kick boxing, and sword fighting. These guys weren't messing – their last fight demonstration featured some very scary-looking weapons. Four-foot-long thin bands of steel whirred back and forth and only incredible dexterity and timing by the performers prevented any loss of body parts. It was heart-in-the-mouth, breathtakingly impressive, and not a pastime Nick or I will be taking up anytime soon.

It just left us with an evening meal to finish the day, and once again Nick had done his homework. We had another meal to remember (gobi Manchurian and mushroom masala), and this time, with a sea view. We should have had our wives with us for such a romantic setting. The only thing that slightly spoilt the scene, with the reflection of the moon dancing on the gently undulating waves, were the huge cranes in the container docks in the background.

We had reached a turning point in our adventure. The next morning, we were going to meet Nick's wife Ellen from the airport. Like our last adventure in northern India, Ellen was going to be with us for our final few days. Things would never be the same. Ellen would bring some much-needed glamour to the party, and our vocabulary, largely based on laddish banter, seaside postcard euphemisms, and sporting clichés, would have to drastically change. It was going to be a trip of two halves, to be fair, but we'd have to take each day as it came.

CHAPTER 9

VENICE OF THE EAST

Alleppey is the old British colonial name for the city that is now officially called Alappuzha. Nick and I always heard it referred to by its old name, and the area we were heading for was commonly referred to as the Alleppey Waterways. This network of picturesque canals, lagoons, and backwaters is what makes the area so unique. If you look at a map of southern India, you'll find Alleppey on the west coast, approximately 650 miles south of Mumbai and 100 miles north of Kanyakumari, the southernmost tip of the Indian mainland.

Although the city's title of 'Venice of the East', might be a little generous, its reputation is founded on a network of connected waterways that might be better described as the 'Norfolk Broads' or 'Everglades' of Kerala. The waterways were formed by the confluence of several rivers, including the Pamba, Achankovil, and Manimala, as they flow into the Arabian Sea, creating a complex ecosystem that supports a rich diversity of flora and fauna. The long history of the region goes back to ancient times, with the waterways playing a crucial role in trade and transportation, particularly during the reign of the Chera dynasty and then later under British colonial rule.

Today, the Alleppey waterways have become a major tourist attraction. Over two million visitors annually come to enjoy the tranquil beauty of the backwaters, experience the local culture, and stay on traditional houseboats called 'kettuvallams'. The houseboats that cruise the waterways were once used to transport rice and spices but have now been converted into luxurious floating hotels with modern amenities, allowing tourists to immerse themselves in the serene beauty of the backwaters while enjoying a unique and comfortable stay. And that's just what we planned to do, but first we had to meet up with Nick's wife, Ellen, at Kochi airport.

Our day began with a 5:30 am call to prayer from a nearby mosque. I don't mind that, I'm normally waking about then anyway and the chanting is a pleasant reminder that you're somewhere abroad and different – although I dare say you could have the same morning alarm call in most large British cities. After paying for our accommodation, and throwing down a quick breakfast, it was time to play taxi roulette again – who would we get this time?

Amal turned out to be a very careful driver (there had to be one). He told us he had many friends in the UK, but when I said, 'Oh really, whereabouts?' he replied, 'In the UK.' He was very complimentary about the British, telling us, 'The British have a very good mind.' Before we had time to fully unpack that one, we were at the world's first fully solar-powered airport. Impressively, Kochi airport uses solar panels to meet all of its electricity needs.

Our boys' adventure was at a turning point. Nick was even wearing a clean shirt. Ellen arrived nearly on time and the three of us made the dash to Alleppey by taxi, arriving just under two hours later at midday. Our houseboat was a traditional Keralan boat that had been converted into a very deluxe waterborne retreat. It had a spacious lounge area, a dining area, an upper-deck viewing lounge, and two comfortable bedrooms, all air-conditioned and fitted out with beautiful wooden furnishings and traditional decor. We were

VENICE OF THE EAST

Alleppey houseboat

underway within seconds of arriving. With our bags stored, we were treated to cool, refreshing cocktails.

The upper deck of the houseboat featured a covered viewing lounge, an ideal spot for watching the world drift by. We spent the afternoon very slowly cruising along the quiet backwaters, relaxing and sipping on cool drinks, taking in the breathtaking scenery... lush green landscapes, swaying palm trees, and picturesque villages that dotted the shores. With over a thousand other houseboats scattered across these waterways, we weren't alone, but at times it felt like we were, especially when we ventured away from the open-water areas. The gentle rocking of the boat and the soothing sound of the water lapping against the sides created a tranquil atmosphere that felt a million miles from the hurley-burley world that Nick and

I had occupied for the first fifteen days of our trip. It was so relaxing that both Ellen and I dropped off to sleep for an hour. At least she had jet lag as an excuse. The rest of the afternoon seemed to slip past effortlessly as the three of us enjoyed each other's company, shared stories, and simply basked in the beauty of our surroundings.

As the sun began to set, painting the sky in a brilliant array of oranges and pinks, we found a perfect spot to tie up for the evening. It must have been a regular stopping place for the crew because they unwound a very long extension cable off the boat, through some undergrowth, and into a nearby house. The crew prepared a mouth-watering fish-based dinner featuring some giant prawns we'd bought earlier at a waterside village. We savoured the delicious meal and then went back to the upper deck to relax and listen to the gentle sounds of music and children singing in a nearby village. At that point we were thankful that the windows had all been closed because a rich variety of winged wildlife was desperate to get inside to join us, attracted by the lights.

The following morning, we had to be back at our base by 7:30am to allow plenty of time to be driven down the coast to Kollam Junction, where we would be catching the midday train to Madurai. The journey was only around 60 miles, but it can take over three hours, so we wanted to leave plenty of contingency time for getting to the station. Before we went to bed, our boatman reassured us we would be back at base by 7:30 in the morning. He reassured us again at 6:30 the next morning when we had breakfast, and he was still doing so at 7:20 as we slipped our mooring. In India there is a more relaxed interpretation of deadlines than in northern Europe. I'm not even sure if the word 'punctuality' is in their dictionary… but maybe everyone is less stressed because of that.

We arrived back in Alleppey at 7:50 am, at the appropriately named Finishing Point. We were just 102 days too late to witness the thrilling climax of the 2023 Nehru Trophy Boat Race, where snake boats – long, slender vessels with decorated prows resembling a cobra's hood – are propelled by hundreds of energetic rowers in a colourful display of speed, tradition, and regional pride.

I know one shouldn't go by first impressions, but when our taxi arrived, it was covered in dents and scratches. It wasn't exactly a circus car with exploding doors and oval wheels, but that's what came to mind. It didn't inspire confidence. We were very reassured, however, when Vikram, who looked like a cloned brother of the keyboard player from Sparks (the amazing Ron Mael), began our journey south. I thought my first impressions were perhaps right after all when Vikram told us 'Indian roads are a circus.' I was just beginning to think what a steady driver he was when, after just twenty minutes, he ran into the back of a motorcycle at a set of traffic lights. I think the poor bike rider had stopped for some crazy reason… maybe the lights were on red. Fortunately, no one was hurt and the only outcome was a few more scratches on Vikram's car.

Vikram's non-stop commentary to us may have contributed to the incident. His English was quite good and he was making the most of the chance to use it. Like most Indian taxi drivers, multi-tasking was not a problem. At one point, while driving and chatting non-stop, Vikram took Nick's phone and put another 2 gigabytes of data on his SIM card.

As we continued our drive down to Kollam Junction, we witnessed a diverse landscape that captured the essence of southern Kerala. One of the most memorable features along the route was the abundance of roadside fish stalls. The aroma of fresh, and sometimes not so fresh, seafood wafted through the air as we passed numerous vendors displaying their catch of the day. The sight of colourful fishing boats and nets along the shore reminded us of the region's long connection to the Arabian Sea and its thriving fishing industry. As usual, there were many stretches of road either under construction or recently completed. At one point we found ourselves on a long stretch of almost empty dual carriageway. A diverse assortment of vehicles passed by on either side of the central barrier, including the occasional oxen-drawn cart that seemed to belong to a different era.

Throughout the drive, we noticed a significant number of Ayurveda hospitals and clinics dotting the roadside, and even a prominent Ayurvedic nursing college, emphasising Kerala's ancient tradition of Ayurvedic medicine. While Nick, Ellen, and I discussed our experiences in Alleppey, Vikram kept up his non-stop running commentary on the region we were passing through and its culture. As we neared Kollam Junction, the urban landscape grew denser, with larger buildings, bustling markets, and heavy traffic. We had a midday appointment with the Chennai Egmore Express, which would take us to Madurai, one of the oldest cities in India.

Arriving at the station half an hour early, we were pleased to see the train already at the platform, ready for boarding. We quickly found our seats in the air-conditioned compartment. There was a slight problem – the AC wasn't working and it wouldn't get switched on until about ten minutes before departure. We weren't sure where to wait at first – it was a toss-up between the oppressive humid heat of the platform or the oppressive humid heat of the railway carriage. With no air conditioning the stale air in the train loitered menacingly, an unpleasant potpourri of previous sweaty occupants, spices, and the occasional waft of 'essence de toilette'. We waited on the platform.

By the time the train pulled out, the carriages had been cleaned and the AC was a welcome sanctuary from the sticky heat of the Tamil Nadu station platform, upon which only Englishmen and mad dogs could be seen in the unshaded parts.

We settled into our 'Second AC' compartment (the mid-range option containing four berths and comfortable bedding) and spread out on the long seats. There was plenty of room for each of us to lie down if we wanted to, with our luggage next to us. We began our six-and-a-half-hour journey to Madurai. The rhythmic clatter of the wheels against the tracks created a hypnotic backdrop as we watched the landscape unfold outside our window. We resumed our acquaintance with the Western Ghats, the majestic mountain range that we seemed to be following down the western coast of India. They dominated the view for much of the journey south. Lush green forests, punctuated by cascading waterfalls and deep ravines, painted a picturesque scene that gave us constantly changing views.

As we'd become used to by now, life on the train took on a character of its own. Chai vendors made their way through the compartments, their singsong voices calling out 'Chai, chai, garam chai!' (Tea, tea, hot tea!). The aroma of the spiced tea mingled with the other scents in the air, some pleasant… some not so, creating a unique olfactory experience. Passengers from all walks of life filled the compartments, some engrossed in lively conversations, some enjoying elaborate picnics, teenagers in parallel worlds on their phones, and many of the older generation dozing off, lulled by the motion of the train.

As the journey progressed, the skies darkened and the heavens opened up. Nick reminded me that we were in the middle of the Northeast Monsoon season. It explained the heavy clouds and sporadic downpours that punctuated the journey. The Northeast Monsoon, also known as the Retreating or Winter Monsoon, affects southern India from October to December, bringing up to 60 per cent of its annual rainfall. The monsoon season is crucial for agricultural activities in the south, particularly in Tamil Nadu, where it's the primary source of rainfall for the rabi cropping season – the period from October to February, during which crops such as rice, maize, pulses, and oilseeds are sown for harvesting the following spring (March to May).

Inside the train, the sound of the raindrops mingled with the clatter of the wheels, creating a soothing white noise that unsurprisingly lulled me into a much-needed nap. It doesn't take much these days. I managed to sleep for a good two hours of the six-and-a-half-hour journey.

As we approached Madurai, the rain subsided, and the evening sun cast a warm glow over the damp landscape. The city's outskirts came into view, at first a sprawling expanse of low-rise buildings and bustling streets. We gathered our bags and prepared to disembark. The train journey from Kollam Junction to Madurai had been enjoyable. They are definitely part of the travel experience in India, not just a means of getting from one stopover to the next.

We got a taxi to the Hotel Tamil Nadu, which is run by the Tamil Nadu Tourism Development Corporation (TTDC), a state government agency that aims to promote tourism and provide accommodation facilities for tourists. Most of the staff seemed quite young. I know most people are young to me, but these seemed *really* young. And some were disabled. We were told that the TTDC has an inclusive employment policy of giving work to young people and individuals with disabilities in their hotels and restaurants… part of a larger mission to promote social welfare and empowerment alongside its tourism initiatives.

Over our evening meal Nick, Ellen, and I discussed our schedule for the following day. We had one full day and two nights in Madurai. A disrespectfully short time, once again, but we still had to fit in stops at Puducherry and Chennai, on the east coast… there was so much to do and so little time.

CHAPTER 10

GODDESS PARVATI, JASMINE AND A TYRANNOSAURUS REX

Before we could begin our day in Madurai, I received a message from the hotel I'd booked for our stay in Chennai – the very nice one we'd splashed out on because it was the culmination of our three-week adventure. They were calling to say they'd had to close due to severe flooding. With no electricity, they were cancelling bookings for several days. Not ideal, but perhaps another little reminder of the climate change crisis that is slowly unfolding. Finding somewhere else could wait. We had a quick breakfast and were good to go. Madurai awaited us.

According to legend, Madurai earned its name, 'The City of Nectar' when Lord Shiva showered the city with drops of divine nectar (madhuram) from his tangled locks. India does this stuff so well, it's hard to imagine such romantic stories attached to places like Swindon or Macclesfield back home. Madurai, situated on the River Vaigai, is Tamil Nadu's third-largest city, with a 2024 population estimated at over 1.8 million. It's renowned for its rich history, cultural heritage, and magnificent temples. One of the oldest continuously inhabited cities in the world, Madurai has a legacy dating back over 2,500 years. It was the capital of the powerful Pandya dynasty, one of the three great Tamil dynasties that ruled the region in ancient times. The city flourished as a centre of Tamil culture, literature, and learning, and was renowned for its trade and commerce. The Pandya kings were great patrons of the arts and literature, and the city attracted scholars, poets, and artisans from far and wide.

In terms of its economy, Madurai is now a major industrial and educational hub. The city has a thriving textile industry, with numerous spinning mills, weaving units, and garment factories. Other important industries include food processing, IT, and automotive components. Madurai is home to several prestigious educational institutions, including Madurai Kamaraj University and the Madurai Medical College. The city is known as the 'Jasmine City' because of the extensive cultivation of jasmine in the surrounding areas. Its famous flowers are exported worldwide and used in products such as perfumes, oils, and garlands. Tourism also plays a significant role in Madurai's economy and Nick, Ellen, and I were going to add our numbers to the millions of visitors who visit Madurai annually. The Meenakshi Amman Temple alone draws about a million foreign tourists and 10 million domestic tourists every year.

The 17th-century Meenakshi Amman Temple is Madurai's most famous landmark and one of the greatest temples in India. Often referred to as the 'Taj Mahal of southern India' for its cultural significance and grandeur, it is dedicated to Goddess Meenakshi (Parvati) and her consort Lord Sundareswarar (Shiva). The temple is a stunning example of Dravidian architecture, a style named after the indigenous Dravidian people of south India, who have a rich cultural heritage that predates the arrival of the Indo-Aryan people from Central Asia. There are north, south, east, and west sides to the temple, and it's easy to walk around the outside to see all four sides. The temple features towering vimanas and elaborately carved gopuram gateways. In simple terms, a vimana is the central, tower-like structure that rises above the sanctum sanctorum (the innermost shrine) of a Hindu temple, housing the deity. Vimanas symbolise a connection between the earthly realm and the heavens. Gopuram gateways are the imposing pyramid-shaped towers over the temple entrances that mark the way into the temple complex. They have multiple tiers of elaborate carvings and sculptures, marking the transition from the mundane world to the sacred space within. Both elements are integral parts of south Indian temple architecture.

It's the image of these huge pyramidal tower gates, or gopurams, 170 feet (52 metres) high, that you will take away when you visit the Meenakshi Amman Temple. The towering structures are adorned with countless sculpted figures of major deities. Goddess Parvati (Meenakshi) features heavily, of course, because

Meenakshi Temple, Madurai

it's her temple, along with Lord Shiva, Lord Vishnu, Lord Brahma, and their countless avatars and manifestations. The gopurams showcase scenes from famous Hindu epics like the Ramayana and the Mahabharata, serving as a visual guide to morals and lessons central to Hindu philosophy.

As you crick your neck to look up, the sheer number of figures on the gopurams is mesmerising. Estimates suggest there are over 33,000 sculptures adorning the towering gate pyramids. The attention to detail and craftsmanship involved in creating these sculptures makes you stop and wonder at the skill and devotion of the artists who worked on the temple over the centuries. The Meenakshi Amman Temple is one of the most important pilgrimage sites in southern India and it was number one on our list of places to visit in the city.

When our tuk-tuk dropped us off at the temple, we realised just how big the place is; the labyrinthine complex covers an area of 14 acres. The area immediately surrounding the temple is kept traffic free, which gives a pleasant feeling of space… unusual in a city centre. We joined the file of visitors waiting to go through the security barriers. Handing over our phones and bags was fine, but then we hit a problem. Nick's shorts were deemed unacceptable. I've told him that many times, but this time he received official confirmation.

Being a resourceful guy he popped over the road to the nearest fabric shop. For 150 rupees (about £1.50) he bought a very fetching orange sarong. He must have splashed out on the premium service because that price also included bespoke fitting by the shop owner. Back at the temple we queued up in the relevant lines – separate entrances for men and women. At the scanner we then had to remove our shoes and socks and take them back to the phone and bag store. Next time at the scanner, the security men instructed me to dispose of the paper handkerchief in my right pocket. Who knew that was on the list of dangerous items? (Probably my wife, Jan.) Nick didn't get away with it either. He got rumbled with a camera in his waistcoat, so he also had to make one more visit to the phone and bag store. Eventually, all three of us got in, met up, and hired a guide (Ramesh) who took us around the temple complex, meticulously explaining every part as we went.

Inside, the place was filled with devotees. The air was heavy with the fragrance of incense and jasmine, and the sound of prayers and chants echoed through the corridors. It was another Indian sensory experience. As we trailed behind Ramesh, I tried to absorb the temple's awe-inspiring interior while listening to his explanations. However, my attention was constantly drawn to the throngs of devotees, each immersed in their own sacred space. The scene was a curious moving human tide where devotees moved in a purposeful dance, visitors explored with eager but hesitant steps, and a lone dog wandered with canine curiosity.

For Nick, Ellen, and me, visiting the Meenakshi Amman Temple was an opportunity to immerse ourselves in a different culture and explore a living piece of history. For the devotees, the temple held a far more profound meaning. The depth of the worshippers' devotion was etched in their faces and woven through every gesture. In the temple, they sought refuge from the trials of daily life, their prayers whispered like secret pacts – for the blessing of good health, the comfort of safety, and the promise of brighter days ahead. This ancient, hallowed ground was their sanctuary, a divine anchor in a churning world, where they could cast off their burdens and find a moment of serenity in the presence of the gods.

Looking around me, it reminded me of the feeling I had in the Golden Temple in Amritsar and the Mahabodhi Temple at Bodh Gaya. It was a humbling reminder of the power of faith and the enormous significance that these ancient temples still hold for people today.

As we made our way deeper into the temple, we marvelled at the ornate mandapams, or pillared halls, where devotees gathered to pray and perform rituals. The craftsmanship and attention to detail in every aspect of the temple's architecture was simply astounding. I'm not sure how much of the 14-acre complex we saw, but our tour around the numerous halls, shrines, and corridors lasted well over an hour. We visited the main shrines dedicated to Goddess Meenakshi and Lord Sundareswarar, explored the Thousand Pillar Hall, admired countless intricate sculptures and paintings, and learnt about the temple's history and significance. My internal-memory hard drive was full well before we'd finished the tour and by then I could sense things were falling out, almost before they'd been consciously registered and filed away for future retrieval.

The Meenakshi Amman Temple was one of the highlights of our three-week trip – a place where history, art, and religion collided in a glorious, slightly chaotic mix. As we stepped out of the temple, our minds still reeling from trying to take it all in, Ramesh, our guide, turned to us with a twinkle in his eye. 'If you thought the temple was a feast for the senses, wait until you see the banana market,' he said with a grin and a wobble of the head. I'm not sure what you're meant to say to that, but we were intrigued by his suggestion, even if it was tongue in cheek. We've seen a few banana markets in our time, so we'd need something special to make us go out of our way for another one, but Ramesh explained it was a must-visit destination for banana lovers and tourists alike – and it was only a stone's throw away. As Ellen hadn't seen the banana market in Mysuru, and they're thin on the ground in the Highlands of Scotland, we thought we'd take a very quick look. Ramesh took us to the iconic statue of Nandi, Shiva's bull, near the East Tower of the temple, from where the market was a five-minute walk.

The wholesale banana market is a bustling blur of colourful activity (mostly yellow) with traders bringing in sixteen different varieties of bananas in massive quantities every morning. To fully immerse yourself in this quintessential Madurai experience, don't do what we did – instead, arrive at 6:00 am, when the market opens, and prepare to be amazed by the sheer volume and variety of curved yellow fruit on display. Visitors can witness the impressive sight of workers unloading and carrying dozens of banana branches into the shops, where they are displayed or hung in clustered form. We took a fairly rapid walk through and then got a tuk-tuk to our next essential Madurai sight.

Madurai is one of the few cities in India with a temple dedicated to Mahatma Gandhi. The Gandhi Memorial Museum, which was our next destination, includes a unique temple where visitors can offer prayers to the Father of the Nation. After the contrasting sensory experiences of the Meenakshi Amman Temple and the banana market, we made our way to the museum, hoping for something a little less frantic. It seemed like the perfect place to calm down and learn more about Gandhi's life and legacy.

The museum, located in the heart of Madurai, attracts around half a million visitors annually, and is housed in a beautiful 17th-century building known as Tamukkam Palace, which was once the residence of Rani Mangammal, a powerful queen of the Nayak dynasty. As we entered the museum complex, we were indeed entering a calm and serene atmosphere, a stark contrast to the bustling streets outside. The well-manicured lawns and the pristine white buildings seemed to emanate a sense of peace and tranquillity, perfectly in keeping with Gandhi's philosophy of 'ahimsa'. The word means 'non-violence' or 'non-injury', and was a core principle in Gandhi's fight for Indian independence. He believed in non-violent resistance against British rule, advocating for civil disobedience, protests, and boycotts to achieve his goals. Gandhi's adoption of ahimsa gained international recognition and continues to inspire movements for peace and social justice around the world. Readers may recognise the word from the world of yoga. Ahimsa is also one of the five Yamas (Ethical Restraints), which form one of the eight limbs of yoga.

We learned that the museum was established in 1959, just eleven years after Gandhi's assassination. It commemorates his life and his role in India's struggle for independence. The museum's collection includes photographs, manuscripts, and belongings of Gandhi, but a large part of the exhibition appeared to trace the history of India's freedom movement. One of the most moving exhibits was a replica of the room in which Gandhi stayed during his visits to Madurai. The simple, spartan furnishings and the spinning wheel in the corner were poignant reminders of a life of simplicity and self-reliance. After Gandhi's assassination, his ashes were divided and sent across the country. Some were immersed in holy rivers, while others were preserved in museums and memorials, including the Gandhi Memorial Museum in Madurai, the Aga Khan Palace

– which Nick and I had visited in Pune – and the Gandhi Smarak Sangrahalaya in Ahmedabad.

As we concluded our visit, we made a stop at the museum's bookshop. While Ellen and I became lost among an extensive collection of books on Gandhi, Indian history, and philosophy inside the bookshop, outside, Nick was becoming acquainted with a life-size model of a Tyrannosaurus rex. It stood incongruously among a collection of centuries-old carvings. Anywhere else you might have thought that a bit odd, but this was India.

Our fleeting glimpse of the city was nearly over, but if you have more time there, two more sites to add to your list are the Thirumalai Nayakkar Mahal, and the Vandiyur Mariamman Teppakulam. The first is a 17th-century palace, renowned for its unique blend of Dravidian and Islamic architectural styles, featuring grand pillars, intricate stucco work, and spacious courtyards that showcase the grandeur and opulence of the Nayak dynasty. The second is a massive temple tank that hosts a spectacular float festival during the Tamil month of Thai (January–February).

That evening, the three of us dined in the rooftop restaurant of the Madurai Hotel Residency in the city centre. Our visit, and another magnificent meal, coincided with another diner's birthday party, and once we'd joined in with their singing of 'Happy Birthday', we became part of the party – lots more photos. Returning to our hotel, we were asked if we wouldn't mind moving into one room for the night. We explained that we were good friends, but we'd rather stay in the two rooms we already had, please. There was much friendly negotiating, after which we were eventually allowed to stay in the rooms we'd occupied the previous night. We'd hoped to collect our freshly washed laundry that evening as promised, but for some reason, there was a delay. We were reassured it would be ready for collection first thing next morning. You can probably tell where this is going.

It had been a long hot and sticky day, and my advice would be to allow at least two days for the city, even for a flying visit. Three or more would, of course, be better. If you're touring southern India, Madurai is a must-visit destination that will leave you awestruck with its ancient temples, colourful markets, and rich cultural heritage – a perfect blend of history, spirituality, and sensory delights that will make you, like us, wonder why you didn't stay longer. The city had exceeded our expectations, but the next day we would be moving on again. Poor Ellen would just about have recovered from her jet lag by the time we got to Chennai to fly home. Next, we were travelling by train again, across country to Puducherry, on the east coast.

CHAPTER 11

FARE FORWARD VOYAGERS... BUT DON'T BE LATE

Anyone travelling through India should expect the odd hiccup. It's built into the very definition of the venture. Consider it character building. One should attempt to minimise the risks, however, by not making too many cock-ups oneself.

I'd slept soundly all night, content in the knowledge I'd be enjoying a leisurely morning in Madurai and a relaxed departure from its railway station at midday. I awoke early, however, and being slightly paranoid about these things, I took a mental meander through the plan and timetable for the day ahead.

At 6:55 am, I checked the train tickets again to confirm our departure time… over-thinking it maybe, but I like to be sure. The departure time '7:50 am' stared back at me derisively, as if to say, 'Not feeling so smug about Indian punctuality now, are we, old chap?' We had less than an hour to get to the station before our train vanished down the line without us. I felt lightheaded.

Being a seasoned traveller, well used to calmly adapting to minor logistical changes in challenging environments… I went into a blind panic. Thoughts and plans dashed around inside my head like a troop of rampaging Maratha cavalrymen. Some of them were mockingly waving freshly laundered items of underwear at me – what the hell was all that about? It was like a very bad dream.

I'm not sure how many times I needed to check the ticket before reality sank in, but with the minutes ticking away, I had to get my anxiety attack under control and come up with plans B to Z. Attention and intention are apparently the keys to creating strong memories; I'd clearly not been paying enough attention, even though I'd intended to. I woke Nick and Ellen in the room next door. They took the early-morning news remarkably well I thought. Just to be sure, I got them to check the train time as well, and then we all set about making a rapid departure from the hotel.

At that moment, our freshly laundered clothes, the ones we were told we would have returned the previous evening, were smelling sweet and lying crisply folded somewhere in a laundry on the other side of Madurai. The startled young man on the hotel reception desk tried his best to simultaneously check us out of the hotel while articulating the options for how we might be reunited with those clean and immaculately folded garments. The discussion could have taken a long time, and I began to worry that it might necessitate a visa extension. We opted instead for the speedy checkout and embarrassed exit strategy, backing out of the hotel lobby, still stuffing things into rucksack pockets, as we concluded the discussion on laundry with the poor bemused guy on the reception desk. How on earth did India cope with the Brits running the place for two hundred years?

In the event, we arrived at the station with twenty minutes to spare. No problem. It was the right train, and we had the right seats – all was well, we were back on track again. Ellen questioned how Nick and I had survived for so long unsupervised up to that point.

The train journey was a surprise, but no surprise there. For the first time, we had the luxury of travelling AC1 executive class, complete with comfortable reclining chairs, ample legroom, large windows, and air conditioning. The sleek modern design was more like a European intercity train than the usual smoke-belching diesel behemoths that Nick and I considered our second home while in India. The seats even swivelled through 360 degrees, allowing passengers to align themselves with the windows to admire the passing scenery more comfortably. Our tickets, in that clinically clean carriage, included an impressive list of extras, but the staff handing out the newspapers and serving meals seemed rather cold and functional, perhaps still awaiting the dates for their customer service training. That line of thinking came to a shuddering halt on the buffers when I reminded myself of the privileged viewpoint from which I was making the observation. I felt guilty about my knee-jerk reaction when I worked out that the cost of my three-week jaunt around their country might have equalled three or four months of their annual salary.

As we journeyed through the lush Tamil Nadu countryside, I found myself once again reflecting on how much train travel shapes the lives of Indian people and how it was contributing to our experience of India. The tentacles of India's sprawling rail network, one of the world's largest, connect a vast nation, uniting a multitude of cultures and languages. Around 1.4 million employees operate over 13,000 passenger trains daily, carrying over 23 million passengers – roughly the equivalent of the entire world's population travelling on Indian Railways in a year.

You might think most of them are in your carriage if you choose the Unreserved Second Class, also known as the General Compartment or Second Class (Sitting), during peak travel times such as festivals or holidays. You've seen the scenes on television – people crammed together like sardines, sitting on the carriage roof, or hanging from the doors. If you want to experience India up close – perhaps closer than you'd expect – this is the ticket class for you. It's not for the faint-hearted, as the lack of personal space can be overwhelming for those unaccustomed to it.

Our usual AC2 ticket class is the Goldilocks choice among the eight available options, offering a perfect balance between socialising with fellow passengers and retreating to the comfort of a cool, private berth when needed.

On our journey towards Puducherry (formerly known as Pondicherry) our AC1 executive seats felt a world away from what we'd become accustomed to on Indian Railways. Life among the business executives with their laptops somehow didn't feel right. For Nick and me our train journeys had become much more than getting from A to B. We often looked forward to getting back on the train, finding it a chance to rest and recuperate. Lethargic clickety-clack progress across an ever-changing landscape provides time for conversation and reflection. You see people from different socio-economic backgrounds, castes, and religions coming together, often sharing food, stories, and experiences – people who might never otherwise meet – yet there they are, sharing a common journey. And then there's the chance to simply gaze at the passing scenery. Declaring an interest, those long, slow journeys also offer a welcome opportunity for sleep and serve as a cheap overnight stay.

The train from Madurai towards Puducherry offered a pleasant touch of luxury, and it was certainly good to experience it. But as we sped towards our destination in hushed and clean efficiency, I found myself already looking forward to the return to those majestic, clanking, old-fashioned trains we'd grown accustomed to. Perhaps Brits of a certain age harbour nostalgic memories of imperious steam locomotives and their oil-stained successors, the diesel leviathans that slowly criss-cross the nation, day and night. A smooth intercity train is like a quickly swallowed, nutritionally efficient multivitamin pill compared to the mixed vegetable biryani with mango chutney and lime pickle of a smoke-belching diesel train.

As we admired the changing landscape, radiant shafts of sunlight pierced through sporadic gaps in the menacing dark monsoon clouds, dramatically illuminating favoured patches in a quilt of paddy fields, coconut palms, and agricultural crops. A wide, level plateau stretched as far as the eye could see, occasionally interrupted by small ridges and isolated hills. As the rain pelted against the panoramic windows once more, the view outside blurred into a wash of colours. We were in the grip of the secondary monsoon, with winds from the northeast picking up moisture from the Bay of Bengal and depositing it generously across southern India – but mostly on our train.

With some spare time for reading, I turned to my copy of the Bhagavad Gita, a sacred Hindu scripture of immense importance in philosophical literature – not just Indian philosophy. I felt I should at least attempt to read and perhaps even understand it a bit. The Gita is centred around a dialogue between the warrior Arjuna and Lord Krishna, one of the principal deities of the Hindu Trimurti (trinity), alongside Brahma and Shiva. The text emphasises fulfilling one's duties without attachment to outcomes (Nishkama Karma), maintaining a balanced and composed mind (Samatva), and surrendering to the Divine. The Bhagavad Gita, or simply 'The Gita', as it is often called, has shaped Indian thought, spirituality, and culture for over two millennia. Spiritual seekers, philosophers, and scholars worldwide have attempted to grasp its teachings. It inspired and guided Mahatma Gandhi, who referred to it as his 'spiritual dictionary', finding solace in its teachings during his struggles. Renowned physicist J. Robert Oppenheimer, often called the 'father of the atomic bomb', famously quoted the Gita after witnessing the first nuclear test, reciting, 'Now I am become Death, the destroyer of worlds', a reference to Chapter 11, Verse 32, where Krishna reveals his divine form to Arjuna. T.S. Eliot, one of the most influential poets of the 20th century, also drew inspiration from the Gita in his poem 'The Dry Salvages', part of his 'Four Quartets'. The line 'Fare forward, voyagers… This is your real destination', echoes Krishna's advice to Arjuna, urging him to move forward without fear and accept life's uncertainties. Nick and I might do well to adopt that as our new travel motto.

As that train of thought continued to rumble down the line, my philosophical musings were interrupted by the sight of wild peacocks wandering across the landscape. This came as a bit of a jolt. I don't know why I hadn't considered them living in the wild, but it seems they're not just confined to stately homes, botanical gardens, and Bangor High Street in North Wales. The vibrant plumage of the exotic-looking beauties was a colourful contrast to the standard white of the more common egrets that were randomly sprinkled among the many paddy fields we were passing.

We crossed the wide Kaveri River, and the landscape changed again, revealing expansive banana plantations and clumps of elephant grass, lemongrass, and tall bamboo groves swaying gently in the soft, warm breeze. Our four-hour journey seemed to go in a flash, and before we knew it, we were slowing down to a halt at Villupuram Junction station, from where we took a taxi to Puducherry, just twenty-five miles away.

Puducherry is another reminder of the historical power grab that took place between the 16th and 19th centuries as European countries spread their resource-snatching tentacles around the globe. England, France, Portugal, the Netherlands, and Denmark all established colonies and trading posts in India. Like moths to a flame, they were drawn to its rich resources, vulnerability, lucrative trade opportunities, and strategic location. The competition for control over India shaped the political, economic, and social landscape of the whole subcontinent during the colonial era. Although the British East India Company, later replaced by the British Crown, became the dominant colonial power, the French and Portuguese, in particular, also had significant territorial possessions. There was even a French East India Company that established trading posts in Surat (1668) and Pondicherry (1674).

Although the French lost most of their territories to the British by the end of the Seven Years' War in 1763, Puducherry remains a reminder of what might have been. Had history taken a different turn, Indians might now be enjoying fine wine while navigating the occasional air traffic control strike, rather than sipping tea while excelling at cricket. French could have been the dominant language for 1.4 billion people, who might have had a few more layers of charmingly intricate bureaucracy to contend with. Bollywood might even be rocking to an accordion beat – though, on second thoughts, perhaps that's pushing it a bit too far.

We were heading for Puducherry's charming French Quarter, where we were booked in to the beautiful and welcoming Gratitude Guest House. Puducherry's distinct character, shaped by its colonial past and vibrant spiritual present, had made it an essential stop for our south India itinerary.

The city lies approximately 160 kilometres (100 miles) south of Chennai, on the south-eastern coast of India. Bordered by the state of Tamil Nadu, Puducherry is a Union Territory. That means it's an administrative division directly governed by the central government of India, unlike states, which have their own elected governments. Looking out over the turquoise waters of the Bay of Bengal, the city is famous for its beaches, such as Promenade Beach, Paradise Beach, and Auroville Beach. They may be famous, but our only encounter with them was a brief walk along the unimaginatively named Puducherry Beach, which was quite dirty and packed with people standing around taking photos of themselves and each other.

With a population of around one million, the city is similar in size to Jodhpur or Amritsar. It was a French colony for nearly three centuries, and the influence of French culture is clear to see in the city's architecture, urban planning, and cuisine. The French Quarter, also known as 'White Town', is relatively petite, but it has charming cobblestone streets, colourful colonial buildings, and French-style cafes and restaurants. Puducherry is one of the few places in India where you can find authentic French bakeries and restaurants. French urban planning has resulted in a grid pattern of perpendicular streets running north-south and east-west, which you don't see elsewhere in India. The rest of the city is like most other medium-sized Indian cities… hot, overcrowded, and chaotic.

Alongside its French influence and sandy beaches, the city's spiritual and yogic heritage is another cornerstone of its international appeal. Puducherry has become a magnet for spiritual seekers, yoga practitioners, and those drawn to alternative lifestyles, mainly thanks to three renowned institutions: the Sri Aurobindo Ashram, Auroville, and the International Centre for Yoga Education and

Research. We planned to visit two of these, but first, we needed to find our accommodation for the night.

Our tuk-tuk driver dropped us near the seafront, in a tranquil oasis nestled within the heart of the old French Quarter. We checked into the charming Gratitude Guest House, an enchanting apricot-coloured colonial residence dating back to the early 1700s. Its tall columns, wide arches, shady inner courtyard, and traditional Madras terrace roof combine to create a heritage homestay of great character and style. With just nine private, en-suite bedrooms, each one unique and delightful, it offered us a perfect retreat.

Saranya gave us a warm welcome as we checked in and she couldn't do enough for us to ensure our comfort. Intentionally or not, our journey through southern India seemed to regularly bump into yogic connections, and here was another one. In the guest house office was an enormous portrait of a young Sri Aurobindo. He was an Indian philosopher, yogi, guru, and poet who devised a spiritual practice he called Integral Yoga. The Sri Aurobindo Ashram he founded in Puducherry in 1926 became a centre for spiritual and cultural activities, and his influence on the city was profound, as we discovered later.

Former guests at the Gratitude include the celebrity cast of the BBC *Real Marigold Hotel* TV series (2020). Nick and Ellen learnt they would be staying in the room once occupied by Dame Zandra Rhodes and I was staying in the bedroom previously occupied by Susie Blake. Saranya recommended the nearby Coromandel Cafe for dinner, and we wandered down the street to enjoy a cool beer and make a dinner reservation for that evening. We were probably walking in the footsteps of Henry Blofeld and his other 'dear old things'… Britt Ekland, John Altman, Paul Chuckle,

Duncan Ballantyne, and Barbara Dickson. We walked into the bar like a comedy cliché looking for a punchline – an Englishman, a Welshman and a Scotswoman. The cafe was very stylish and comfortable… It wouldn't have taken much to tempt us to stay longer but we didn't have long in town anyway, so we thought we should take a look around.

After a five-minute stroll to the beach in the late-afternoon sun we were relieved to cool off with a paddle in the Bay of Bengal. Although 'Pondy' beach was sandy and pleasant, there was a noticeable amount of dirt and litter. We saw several people contributing to this, which seemed to be completely normal behaviour. There were none of the sun-bathing, swimming, or beach game activities you might expect to see on a typical summer's day in Bournemouth or Blackpool. There was not a single sand castle, donkey, or paddleboard to be seen. No deck chairs, knotted handkerchiefs, or red raw sunburnt bodies. Everyone there (all Indian) just seemed to stand around, well covered up, chatting in groups or couples. Young flirting couples and older mums and dads adopted a series of stereotypical Bollywood-type poses as they spent most of their time taking photos. Men had to fold their arms and look serious and brooding as they thrust out their chests. Women had to toss back their hair and maybe hold the back of a hand against their forehead while simultaneously attempting to beam a smile and look vulnerable. Large sunglasses were mandatory. A small army of trinket sellers sold an endless supply of cheap toys to keep young children amused. We eventually wandered back to the hotel via the French War Memorial, a poignant reminder of the soldiers who lost their lives during World War I.

Over a delightful meal at the chic and stylish Coromandel Cafe, an old French colonial building with furniture and decor to match, we reflected on the day and discussed the city's unusual blend of cultures. We experienced another communication misunderstanding when I asked the waiter how many people the sharing platter was for. 'It's just for one,' came the snappy reply. I might be slightly pedantic but if that was back in Britain, I'd have questioned it. Somehow, being in India, I just accepted it. It was probably my fault for not asking in French.

The next morning, as the half-light of a new Puducherry dawn was turning to day, I was up in time to attend a drop-in yoga class at the Karma Cultural Centre. Well, that was the plan, but it didn't quite work out that way. I mistakenly thought the guest house security man, the only person around at 6:00 am, had been briefed to arrange a tuk-tuk for me when I appeared. He seemed to know nothing about it, and with an almost total language barrier, I began a mental trawl through a range of alternative plans. I had a quick search on the internet for 'Karma Cultural Centre' and found nine listed in Puducherry... great. I walked towards the nearest one; surely that would be the one. Ten minutes later I arrived at the spot, there was nothing resembling a yoga class there, or even a building. I gave up and went back to the guest house. Instead of a downward-facing dog, I enjoyed a pleasant breakfast with Nick and Ellen in the hotel's dining room, which opens onto the most picturesque shaded courtyard. Ellen received a message from an old friend recommending a visit to Auroville, an experimental township located about 12 miles north of Puducherry. It was already on our shortlist of places to visit, but the message elevated it to our new number one and after breakfast we set off to explore. I'm so glad we did.

It was still relatively early when we left the cool embrace of the guest house and headed out into an already hot and sticky Puducherry morning. That's how I remember Pondy, probably the nearest to uncomfortable I became on our southern Indian tour. The city enjoys a tropical climate, with relatively high average temperatures throughout the year in a fairly narrow range between 25°C in December to 33°C in June. It felt very humid to me, although by Indian standards I think it was quite average.

Our short ride to Auroville felt refreshingly cool because an open-sided tuk-tuk comes with built-in air conditioning. Our journey took us through the complete spectrum of the city's architecture, from gallic chic, past dilapidated but once fashionable banlieue, through overcrowded commercial chaos, and into the squalor of out-of-town semi-slums. A long section of road on the northern outskirts was dedicated to demolition recycling shops. Propped up outside were magnificent ornate doorways, windows, and statues, presumably salvaged from old temples. Like a montage of forgotten dreams, rows of old teak and rosewood doors hinted at secrets and surprises behind every weathered facade.

Auroville is unusual. I've not seen anything quite like it. It's an experimental township founded over 50 years ago by Mirra Alfassa, a charismatic French woman also known as 'The Mother'. She was a spiritual collaborator of Sri Aurobindo, who we met back at the guest house. Born Aurobindo Ghose in 1872 in Calcutta (now

Kolkata), Sri Aurobindo was a key figure in India's independence movement before becoming a spiritual reformer.

Mirra Alfassa was born in Paris in 1878. A seeker of spiritual purpose, she became attracted to the teachings of Sri Aurobindo. They began corresponding, and a shared spiritual connection developed. In 1914, Mirra married Paul Richard, a French lawyer and politician who had been appointed as a professor at the newly established French University in Puducherry, then a French colony. Mirra accompanied her husband to Puducherry, where she met Sri Aurobindo. That seems a remarkable coincidence.

It was a turning point in both their lives. Mirra had found the spiritual guru she had been seeking, and Sri Aurobindo had found an influential collaborator. Mirra returned to France with her husband at the outbreak of World War I, but she returned to Puducherry in 1920 to join Sri Aurobindo in his spiritual work, becoming known as 'The Mother'. Together, Sri Aurobindo and The Mother developed the concept of Integral Yoga, a comprehensive spiritual practice that aims to integrate yogic principles into all aspects of an individual's life. The goal of Integral Yoga is to attain higher levels of consciousness, enabling a complete unity with the divine and a profound understanding of the true nature of reality. That sounded very similar to the aims of the Isha Foundation.

In 1926 the couple founded the Sri Aurobindo Ashram in Puducherry. It was a place where spiritual seekers could live and work together, focusing on their spiritual growth and the practice of Integral Yoga. As Sri Aurobindo gradually withdrew from public life to focus on his spiritual work and his writings, The Mother took over management of the ashram's daily operations and grew the Sri Aurobindo Ashram into a large spiritual community, attracting people from all over the world. When Sri Aurobindo passed away in 1950, his philosophical and spiritual legacy continued through The Mother's work and the ashram. The Mother had big ideas, however, bigger than the ashram could accommodate, and in 1968 she founded Auroville.

The township of Auroville, sometimes referred to as 'The City of Dawn', was designed to be a city of 50,000 people, where inhabitants from all nations could live together in peace and harmony. Spread over an area of approximately 20 square kilometres (7.7 square miles), Auroville has grown from a handful of hippy-like pioneers to a diverse and functioning community of around 3,500 inhabitants from over 60 countries. Although there are more than half a dozen such 'intentional communities' around the world with similar aspirations, Auroville is one of the largest, with its own infrastructure, economy, and governance. It has been endorsed by UNESCO and is supported by the government of India. Residents are guided by the Auroville Charter, founded on the spiritual principles of Sri Aurobindo and The Mother.

Seen from above the township looks like an eye, staring out from the earth's surface into the universe. At the heart of its 'sacred geometry' lies the Matrimandir, a large spherical structure covered in golden discs, symbolising the sun's rays. Inside the dome is a large meditation hall known as the Inner Chamber, which is devoid of any religious symbols and serves as a space for individuals to meditate and connect with their inner selves. In that respect, it seems to serve a similar purpose to the Dhyanalinga meditative space at the Isha Foundation in Coimbatore.

The iconic structure of the Matrimandir, considered the 'soul of the city', is situated within the oval-shaped Peace Area, encircled by a

The Matrimandir, Auroville

tranquil lake. The township radiates outward from the lake, divided into Industrial, Cultural, Residential, and International zones, each focusing on a crucial aspect of Auroville's life. Surrounding the entire township is the Green Belt, a lush expanse comprising forested areas, farms, and sanctuaries. Three million trees planted around the township are a statement of the township's commitment to sustainability, as well as acting as a natural buffer to the world beyond. Aiming for a lifestyle of simplicity, sustainability, and spiritual growth, the community residents, known as Aurovillians, aim to be self-sufficient in terms of food, energy, and water. They have implemented various eco-friendly practices such as organic farming, solar power, and water conservation.

What's not to like? A peace-loving community free from man-made national and religious constructs, working harmoniously together for mutual benefit – is that even possible? What's the catch?

Our tuk-tuk driver dropped us off at the Auroville visitor car park and we agreed to be back with him in two hours. Visitors are free to wander around the township, and there is an excellent exhibition centre. Although it is possible to visit the Matrimandir, prior booking of at least a day or two is required. Two hours to look around felt about right.

The history, philosophy, aims, principles, and way of life of Auroville are all very well described in its excellent visitor centre. I became confused by the potential contradiction between the community's emphasis on 'no religion' and the frequent references to the Divine and the Lord. I sought clarification. The two Indian people manning the sales desk were presumably locals employed by the Aurovillians, and they seemed more comfortable selling books than trying to answer philosophical questions from a weird foreigner. I guess the answer is that the Aurovillians believe in a divine spiritual consciousness, but not in the concept of organised religion.

I thought I'd make the two staff members feel more comfortable by buying a book, *A House for the Third Millennium: Essays on Matrimandir*, not realising the cultural tsunami I was about to unleash. As I handed over the money – with my left hand – the two Indians behind the desk visibly recoiled in disapproval.

'Oh, I'm so sorry, is that not correct?' I asked. 'Should I pay with my right hand… Is it like eating food with the right hand only?'

'Yes, sir, you must use the right hand only; the left hand is unclean.'

I didn't want to appear confrontational, but I was intrigued. 'But about 10 per cent of the world's population are left-handed,' I said. 'Surely that's the case in India as well, isn't it? What do those people do?'

'It is beaten out of any children who show signs of being left-handed,' came the reply, with the merest hint of a smile and a slight wobble of the head.

This time, it was my turn to raise my eyebrows in surprise. I risked pushing the topic further by adding, 'But I'm left-handed, so for me it's my right hand that's "unclean" – the one I use for certain hygienic purposes.'

My simultaneous hand gesture was a step too far. They both gasped again, and one of them threw his hands up to cover his eyes, shouting, 'Oh no.'

They seemed genuinely shocked. 'Oh, shit,' I thought. I hoped I hadn't offended them.

For a moment, I considered sharing the latest advances in Smart Hygiene Intelligent Toilet technology with them. The concept of 'hands-free' toileting could potentially ease some of the cultural challenges that left-handers like me face in India. The idea of hands-free functionality combined with health monitoring features, like heart rate and stool consistency, certainly takes personalisation to a new level. While facial recognition is one thing (and faecial recognition something else), the prospect of technology tracking more intimate aspects of our lives is both intriguing and a bit unsettling, depending on your perspective. Then there's the question of data privacy. As smart toilets edge their way into the wellness tech market, one has to wonder – what if someone hacked into such sensitive data? It's incredibly personal information at stake here – that's the bottom line. But on reflection, I decided to keep these thoughts to myself, realising I might have been wading into a more sensitive subject than anticipated.

Taking my change – in my right hand, of course, the unclean one – I thanked the two people behind the desk profusely and backed away. While my mind went through a long list of tasteless toilet puns, I went in search of Nick and Ellen. I was perhaps subconsciously looking for safety in numbers in case another international incident was brewing.

After a twenty-five-minute leisurely walk in sweltering heat, we reached a spot where we had a good view of the Matrimandir. Although we could only admire it from a distance, it was quite a sight. It's a huge metallic gold sphere, like a 36-metre-diameter golf ball sitting on a raised platform, that acts as a tee. Surrounded by beautiful gardens, the sphere is covered with 1,415 gold-plated discs that reflect the sunlight, creating a radiant effect.

This is a serious piece of 'spiritual architecture'. The Matrimandir took 37 years to construct, from the laying of the foundation stone in 1971 to its completion in 2008, and in its inner chamber I'm told you can find the world's largest optically perfect glass globe, measuring 70 centimetres in diameter. Sunlight directed onto the globe creates a beam of light that is said to illuminate the interior space. It is not a temple in the traditional sense. The building is designed as a place for spiritual contemplation and individual silent concentration.

Standing in the viewing area, looking out over construction work for an enormous lake or canal, Nick, Ellen, and I got chatting with other visitors, and exchanged views on the township and the globe. We had a fascinating discussion with a wealthy millennial

Indian traveller and a Tibetan monk. That's an interesting combination. We came across them discussing Buddhist beliefs and joined in. It's the sort of conversation you want to remember, and afterwards, as soon as I could, I wrote a few lines down, as best as I could remember them. The Indian woman was very well travelled considering her relatively young age and was clearly very sceptical about the whole yogic township thing. She couldn't see how it could work in the long run given human nature. 'Look how we've screwed up the planet so far' I remember her saying, and then, 'is the model really scalable?... Can these guys ever truly integrate with the local community and culture? I don't think so.' The quietly spoken monk was more optimistic, admiring the determination of the Aurovillians to work as a community as they try to find a collective path to enlightenment. It's the sort of conversation you want to explore further, slowly and thoughtfully, late into the night and possibly with a few glasses of scotch for greater clarity. Nothing was resolved or concluded of course, but in that brief exchange they seemed to articulate a perfect summary of the Auroville experiment – it was one of profound ambition and admirable aims, but so difficult to achieve in practice. One very practical result of the discussion, however, on a lighter note, was a recommendation to visit the Fort St George Museum in Chennai.

For all the progress Auroville has made towards sustainable living and community building it has faced predictable challenges and is a long way from The Mother's dream of a city of 50,000 inhabitants living a collective life, preparing the way towards a brighter future for the whole planet... 'a place where all human beings of good will, sincere in their aspiration, could live freely as citizens of the world, obeying one single authority, that of the supreme truth.'

The reality has involved internal conflicts, integration difficulties with the local population, and controversies over land ownership and development plans. Recent events, such as protests against deforestation for road construction and a sexual abuse scandal exposed by the BBC, have cast more shadows and further hampered Auroville's journey towards its goals. Some observers fear that Aurobindo's philosophy of Integral Yoga is being co-opted for political purposes by the ruling BJP party.

While Auroville's struggles highlight how difficult it is to create a harmonious society, it still offers hope for a more enlightened way of living, despite the competitive and selfish behaviour hardwired into human nature... The township is a bold and admirable vision and who wouldn't want them to succeed?

Like all the places we were visiting, it was impossible to get a proper in-depth appreciation of Auroville in the time we had. Our judgements can only be initial impressions. I would love to go back to Auroville and other places we'd visited, like RIMYI and the Isha Foundation, for example, to volunteer for a few weeks or more to get a more balanced view of what they really represent. Our wander around Auroville took almost exactly two hours. It was as if the taxi driver had been there before and knew how long we'd need.

Back in Puducherry, we enjoyed a late lunch on another rooftop restaurant discovered through Nick's diligent research. Our lofty vantage point meant we were entertained by parents picking up their schoolchildren from the school across the road. Most of the kids were whisked away on motorbikes – sometimes with three or four precariously balanced on a single vehicle. No wonder they grow up with no fear of Indian roads.

After lunch and a quick freshen up back in the guest house, we headed for the Aurobindo Ashram. The afternoon sun beat down on us; it was perhaps the hottest and stickiest I had felt in India. With cool marble floors and a tranquil atmosphere, the ashram offered a brief respite from that heat. In the reception area, we were greeted by a friendly volunteer who gave us a brief history of the ashram. She provided us with a map and pointed out some key areas of interest, such as the samadhi (tomb) of Sri Aurobindo and The Mother, the meditation hall, and the bookshop. Stepping into the courtyard, the first thing that caught our attention was the large tree in the centre, perhaps because of the shade underneath its branches. The second thing was just how many people were there. Some people sat under the tree reading books, while others were engaged in quiet conversation. Many were meditating, sitting cross-legged on the ground with their eyes closed.

Deciding to begin with the bookshop, I was amazed by the sheer number of books on spirituality, philosophy, and yoga. The shelves were neatly arranged, and the books were in various languages, reflecting the diverse nature of the ashram's visitors. After making a small purchase, I wandered over to the samadhi. The white marble structure was adorned with fresh flowers, and there was an almost tangible feeling of reverence in the air. People stood quietly, some with their hands folded in prayer, while others placed flowers on the samadhi as an offering. As I stood there, taking in the serene ambiance, I noticed an elderly gentleman sitting on a nearby bench. With a long white beard, skin like dark mahogany, and dressed in a simple white dhoti, the Gandhi lookalike must have been 100 years old if he was a day. I didn't want to disturb him, but I couldn't help but wonder what his story was, and his connection with the ashram. He might have been Brian from Bolton for all I knew.

Before leaving, I spent a few moments in the meditation hall, trying my best to sit quietly and cease the fluctuations of my mind. It was difficult in that heat, and with so many things still buzzing around my head waiting to be properly processed and filed. The hall was dimly lit, with a large photograph of Sri Aurobindo and The Mother at the front. I gradually felt myself cooling and calming down. Exiting the Sri Aurobindo Ashram, I felt thankful for the brief glimpse into the spiritual legacy of Sri Aurobindo and The Mother. Though fleeting, it left us all with a sense of appreciation for the experience, and plenty to think about.

It's a fifteen-minute walk from the Sri Aurobindo Ashram to the Manakula Ganpati Temple, one of the oldest shrines in the region. Looking at Nick's diary entry for this walk he dedicates almost three pages to the extended negotiations he had with a particularly determined street vendor. Nick ended up buying a small wire trinket for a bargain price of 100 rupees, having knocked the price down from an initial 700 rupees after an epic battle of minds.

The history of the Manakula Ganpati Temple dates back to the 17th century. It is dedicated to our dear friend Lord Ganesha, without whom our trip would not have been the same. We would almost certainly have missed the 7:50 am train from Madurai to Villupuram Junction without him.

Legend has it that a French soldier once attempted to remove the idol of Lord Ganesha from the temple, but the idol kept reappearing in its original spot; a miracle that led to an even greater reverence for the temple and its deity. The temple's architecture is a blend of traditional Tamil and French colonial styles and inside, the walls are painted with around forty beautiful friezes depicting scenes from Hindu mythology. Lord Ganesha is housed in the main sanctum and here he is known as Manakula Vinayagar, which means 'Ganesha of the sand dunes'. The name goes back to the original construction of the temple when it included a pond surrounded by sand.

Nick, Ellen, and I joined the procession of worshippers and we each received a fire blessing. The temple also houses a smaller shrine dedicated to Lord Murugan, the often overlooked brother of Lord Ganesha. Reunited with our footwear, the three of us became mesmerised by a painting of a linga on the ceiling of the archway outside the temple. Wherever you walk to look at it, the linga is still pointing at you: a powerful visual metaphor for the personal and intimate relationship between the divine and the worshipper. It can be seen as a symbolic representation of the idea that Lord Shiva, as represented by the linga, is always connected to and focused on the devotee... even as they walk under the archway and away from the temple.

Nick had done his research again and found a sea-view rooftop restaurant for our evening meal. The sea breeze was a welcome relief from the lingering warmth of the night. As we dined, the three of us reflected on what had been another extraordinary day on our journey. Puducherry had been a mixed bag for me – Aurobindo and The Mother were unexpected discoveries that left me intrigued by the Auroville experiment. I could have easily stayed at the Gratitude Guest House for months; it was an absolute delight. The French Quarter, with all its charm, was everything I had hoped for, but it was diminutive compared to the sprawling, chaotic city beyond. Puducherry's unique blend of French and Tamil influences had woven its own subplot into the larger narrative of India's rich cultural diversity.

Yet, there was no escaping the oppressive heat and humidity. Perhaps I'm more sensitive to it than most, but Puducherry was the only place in India where I found myself dripping with sweat without even moving. This discomfort turned my thoughts to climate change, a topic of increasing urgency in the world's most populous country and the third-largest emitter of greenhouse gases, after the US and China. India is acutely aware of its responsibilities and has been vocal on the global stage. At the COP27 climate change conference in 2022, Prime Minister Narendra Modi outlined India's aim to reduce emission intensity by 45 per cent by 2030 and to increase the share of non-fossil fuels to 50 per cent, with a particular focus on hydrogen as an alternative fuel.

Climate change is an enormous and complex issue, one of the most critical of our time. While India's historical contribution to global emissions is relatively small – about 3 per cent of the total – it is poised to play a significant role in shaping the future. The vast rural population, many without access to reliable power, highlights the deep inequities and challenges the nation faces. Yet, despite the global significance of these issues, it had often been difficult to think beyond my immediate discomfort in the sweltering streets of Puducherry.

As we enjoyed our final evening in Puducherry, I reflected on the rich diversity we had experienced throughout our journey. Each destination offered a unique glimpse into India's vast history, spirituality, and its rapid march towards the future. Puducherry, with its mix of French colonial charm and Tamil vibrancy, stood as a testament to the enduring influence of cultures across time, while also revealing the challenges of a modernising nation.

The gentle sea breeze reminded me of the contrasts we'd encountered — from the calm of Auroville to the bustling energy of India's cities, and the broader challenges facing the world. Our journey through southern India had been more than a physical adventure; it was a passage through time, culture, and consciousness, leaving much to ponder and appreciate.

As I sipped my tea and watched the waves, I felt deep gratitude for the experiences, lessons, and memories we'd gained.

CHAPTER 12

'COOUM RIVER, WIDER THAN A MILE'

Chennai was formerly known as Madras – a name we'd frequently encountered during our journey through India, often printed after the word 'chicken' on menus. It was the final destination of our three-week tour. Nick, Ellen, and I were hoping to find a city of bold, vibrant flavours, with a perfect balance of heat and tanginess.

Having spent eight weeks touring India over two trips, Chennai marked the end of our adventure… at least for now. During our 2020 visit, Nick and I travelled for five weeks in a large arc across northern India, from Mumbai to Kolkata, with a few detours along the way. This time, we'd swept south from Mumbai, journeyed down and across the country, and ended up in Chennai, on the east coast. Looking at the map, we realised we'd missed a sizeable stretch of the east coast, along with much of the northern and eastern extremities. Those would have to wait for another time.

In reality, we'd only scratched the surface of this vast country, yet we'd somehow chosen a path that provided us with some of the most extraordinary sights and experiences in the world. Chennai was our last fleeting stop, and in keeping with the rest of the trip, we wouldn't be lingering. A visit to the Fort St George Museum, as recommended by the young Indian traveller we met at Auroville, would serve as a fitting conclusion to our tour of the subcontinent, tying together themes of geography, history, colonialism, and cultural identity that we'd encountered along the way.

Chennai, located on the Coromandel Coast of the Bay of Bengal, is the capital city of Tamil Nadu. Originally known as Madraspatnam, the name was derived from 'madras', referring to a fishing village, and 'patnam', meaning town or settlement. The city's development began in earnest in 1639 when the British East India Company chose to establish a trading post there.

The city played a significant role in the Indian independence movement and has since grown into a bustling metropolis, a major economic, cultural, and educational hub with a population of over 10 million. Known as the 'Cultural Capital of South India', Chennai also wears the hat of the 'Detroit of India', thanks to its thriving car industry. In addition, it hosts a diverse range of modern industries, including electronics, information technology, pharmaceuticals, aerospace, and space research. The city is home to major manufacturing plants of companies like Royal Enfield and Hyundai, as well as IT giants such as TCS and Infosys. On the sporting front, the Chennai Super Kings is one of the most successful and consistent cricket teams in the history of the Indian Premier League.

My plan A for Chennai had been set several months before we departed for India. It involved a visit to the Indian Space Research Organisation's Satish Dhawan Space Centre and a tour of the Royal Enfield factory. It also included a 10k run, now our traditional way of closing any tour of India. Visiting the space centre in time for a rocket launch and touring the Royal Enfield factory just as their new model, the Himalayan 450, was being launched in Britain would have been a perfect blend of the old and new in this ancient yet dynamic country. Unfortunately, my one-way correspondence with the space centre and Royal Enfield proved fruitless, and the 10k run was cancelled due to flooding. So, it was on to Plan B.

We left Puducherry in the midst of a brief but violent Northeast Monsoon thunderstorm, grateful to be in a solid car rather than an open-sided tuk-tuk. For a hundred-mile drive to Chennai, a tin shed powered by a lawnmower engine might not have been the most ideal choice anyway. We had planned to go by train but were advised to take a car since there's no station in Puducherry, and we would have had to backtrack over 20 miles to Villupuram Junction to begin the three-to-four-hour train journey to Chennai.

We said au revoir to Puducherry and soon found ourselves heading north on the East Coast Road (ECR). The landscape shifted from quaint colonial to city outskirts to rustic countryside. The road was flanked by lush green paddy fields, swaying palm trees, and the occasional fishing village. The cobalt blue Bay of Bengal appeared intermittently on our right, its foaming white waves crashing against the shore, while on our left were numerous small lakes and waterways, some not so small, swollen from the recent rains.

As usual, the road was filled with an eclectic mix of vehicles – cars, buses, lorries, motorcycles, and carts. They shared two things in common: they were all overloaded and all appeared unroadworthy. Apart from the oxen-pulled carts, which moved at a geological pace in the humid heat, all vehicles sped along at improbable speeds, occupying every available inch of the carriageway, which, for long stretches, was unusually long and straight.

We passed through stretches of road dotted with colourful fruit stalls, small eateries, and local shops selling everything from handicrafts to spare car wheels. The roadside shops became more frequent as we approached Mahabalipuram, a UNESCO World Heritage Site famous for its ancient rock-cut temples and sculptures.

Just before we reached the town, we had to navigate around several improbable-looking coagulations of hardware teetering along the road on two wheels. Imagine a man on a bicycle, now pile the entire contents of an ironmongers shop on top of him – pots, pans, ironing boards, kettles, water carriers, and ladders – and then ask him to ride to the next village. It was like a mobile art installation exploring urban life, consumerism, plumbing, and environmental sustainability. Perhaps it was 'Guinness World Records – most ironmongery you can balance on a bicycle' day. We saw three separate attempts at the record underway. I felt guilty for not stopping to buy a pressure cooker, just to make the poor guys' journey worthwhile.

Around halfway through our journey, the heavens opened, and a biblical downpour reduced visibility to near zero. I was impressed that our driver's car had windscreen wipers – and even more impressed that he was using them. He even slowed down enough to see where he was going! Overall, he was unusually careful. To offset this, and perhaps to give himself a bit of a challenge, he chatted on his mobile phone for the entire three hours and ten minutes of the drive.

The rain brought a refreshing coolness to the air and a vibrant green hue to the surrounding countryside. This might not have been so appreciated by the group of bedraggled racing cyclists we passed. Timing our stop to keep dry, we pulled into a local dhaba (roadside restaurant) for a hot cup of chai and some tasty dosa and bajji snacks. I remember the section of road after our stop because it was unusual. We drove along a long, straight stretch, and for probably the first time in India, our road journey became relatively monotonous. I didn't know that could happen. We rattled off mile after mile through nondescript, flat, and watery countryside blurred by regular downpours.

I slipped into my own private world as I stared blankly at the passing countryside, and my thoughts began to drift. My mind went back to those poor guys on the bikes with the pots and pans. I thought how lucky I was to have been born where I was, when I was, and into the family I was. It takes a while to gain perspective on these things. Travel helps. It makes you realise how many of your day-to-day issues are trivial. The choice of supermarket own-brand recycled or luxury quilted toilet paper is something that probably doesn't stress the occupants of nearly one-third of Indian households that don't have access to toilets within their premises. I have the luxury of a modest pension that allows me to fly halfway around the world just for the fun of it. Millions of people in India live in poverty, just scratching a living. I had the same thoughts last time I was in India; it's difficult not to. I remembered concluding last time that you can't solve those problems for those millions of people. But you can show a little kindness when you can, it will make a difference to someone… and be thankful for what you have… and treasure it. A sudden lurch of the car as we swerved to avoid a broken-down tuk-tuk brought me back to the same world as everyone else in the car.

Further north, around the town of Kalpakkam, we drove past an extensive area of salt pans – a distinctive feature of the coastal landscape and a significant part of the local economy. A glance at the map showed a lot of low-lying wetlands in the lower reaches of the River Palar as it approaches the sea. As the landscape became increasingly urbanised, we could tell we were approaching Chennai. The small towns and villages gradually gave way to larger settlements, industrial areas, and a growing number of high-rise buildings. We passed a nearly empty field with a sign reading: 'Chennai Virtual College'. The traffic intensified as we entered the city limits, with the ECR merging into the bustling IT corridor of Chennai.

Our hotel in central Chennai was modern and comfortable. Once checked in, we set off in search of another restaurant that our team's catering consultant had identified for a spot of lunch. Hang on though, what was that racket heading our way? A cacophony of loud music, singing, and wailing was coming towards us as we crossed the road bridge over the Cooum River. It was a funeral procession, but unlike any we'd seen before. At the centre was a beautifully decorated, motorised carriage with open sides and back. Inside was an open coffin, offering the suited incumbent a splendid view of the joyous scenes around him. The entire vehicle was encrusted with gold and adorned with garlands of green, yellow, and pink flowers. Preceding the carriage was a lively band, filled with musicians playing traditional instruments such as the nadaswaram (a long, wood and brass wind instrument) and the thavil (a barrel-shaped drum). The music was upbeat and joyful, setting the tone for the entire procession, similar to those in New Orleans. I read later that the nadaswaram, traditionally played during major life events, like weddings and funerals, is one of the world's loudest non-brass acoustic instruments.

Among the sizeable crowd of mourners following the procession, someone was carrying a large portrait of the deceased. What struck me most was the sight of so many joyous people dancing and singing around the carriage, all colourfully dressed and celebrating the life of the man in the coffin. Many onlookers joined in, some offering flowers or small gifts, while others simply watched in silent reverence. I wasn't sure whether to bow my head or do a quick samba shuffle. A passer-by must have seen the look of incredulity on our faces and told us that this type of funeral procession is common among the Nadar community in Tamil Nadu, who believe in celebrating the life of the deceased rather than focusing on the sorrow of loss. Good for them… fantastic.

It almost goes without saying that we had another brilliant meal for lunch (Nick's diary reminds me it was Sambar, Prawn Masala, and Paneer Curry). Afterwards, we set off for Marina Beach, which is claimed to be the longest urban beach in India. We were greeted by a vast expanse of flat sand stretching as far as the eye could see – a characteristic you want to see with long beaches. Spanning over 13 kilometres (8 miles), the beach was certainly long. It wasn't particularly clean, but it was alive with activity. Throngs of people from all walks of life, and a single wandering white cow with magnificent black horns, had gathered on the beach. There were loved-up couples, mutually tolerant couples, families enjoying picnics, children playing cricket, and, of course, the omnipresent vendors selling everything from ice cream to kites.

We took a leisurely stroll along the shore, taking in the iconic landmarks of the Mahatma Gandhi statue, the Triumph of Labour sculpture, and the memorial to M.G. Ramachandran. Often referred to as MGR, he was the Chief Minister of Tamil Nadu from 1977 to 1987 and a highly influential figure in Tamil Nadu politics.

We slowly promenaded along the seafront, feeling a bit of mid-afternoon lethargy. When the sun eventually began to set, we decided to head towards the Puratchi Thalaivar Dr M.G. Ramachandran Central Railway Station, which for the sake of brevity we'll call Chennai Central. We didn't have enough time left in the day to visit Fort St George, so we saved that for the next day. Our choice wasn't completely random, however, because Chennai Central is one of the most prominent landmarks in the city, a heritage building, and considered a classic among discerning fans of Indian railway terminals. Built in 1873, and one of the oldest in India, Chennai Central railway station is another magnificent example of Gothic Revival architecture, featuring towering arches, intricate designs, and a grand facade. The nearby Royapuram Station, which began operations in 1856, is the oldest surviving operational railway station on the Indian subcontinent.

With over half a million passengers using its seventeen platforms daily, Chennai Central is one of the busiest railway stations in the country. We wandered inside to tread some of those well-worn platforms, feel the atmosphere, and grab a few photos. The place was, of course, heaving with people – at least half a million, it seemed – and there was a constant hubbub of hustle and bustle. We designated a meet-up spot in case we got separated in the crowds. That must have been Ellen's idea, I can't imagine Nick or me being that thoughtful.

Hundreds of people from all over the country were standing or sitting around, spilling out from arriving trains or hurrying to catch those departing. The air was filled with the heady aroma of diesel fumes, samosas, and chai as trains idled noisily and vendors competed to be heard, making their way through the crowds. There was a nervous energy that made me feel like I'd missed my train, even though I wasn't going anywhere. Perhaps I was still mentally

'COOUM RIVER, WIDER THAN A MILE'

Chennai Central Station

scarred by our early-morning escape from Madurai. We didn't stay long. Our hunger for urban transit experiences remained unsatisfied, however, so we headed back to our hotel via the metro to taste life on the modern Chennai underground.

We descended into the sleek and shiny efficiency of the Chennai Central metro station. It's only five years old, and everything still looks brand new and smells showroom fresh. A friendly commuter helped us to purchase some 20-rupee tickets for the short journey to the Thousand Lights metro station, and we proceeded to the platform to board the air-conditioned coach. It was busy, but not uncomfortably so. We found ourselves among a very diverse crowd, including office workers, students, and families. Several of them wanted selfies, of course. The brief journey gave us a glimpse of a completely different environment to the one above. This one was cool, slick, shiny, and efficient. It couldn't be more different from the hot, ramshackle, and chaotic world above. We alighted at the metro station named after the iconic Thousand Lights Mosque and made our way back to the surface. Returning to the 'normal' India at ground level, we took the short walk to our hotel.

Before I was really ready for it, our last full day in India had arrived. We already wanted to come back, even before we'd left. We had plenty of time to visit Fort St George, but first, we had to find our way in. There is minimal public access to most of the Fort St George area of the city because the business of the government of Tamil Nadu takes place daily within many of the buildings. However, one part has been turned into the Fort Museum, and that's where we headed first.

We were directed through a high-security scanner, and on the other side, we were inspected by a man with a hand scanner. When he was quite satisfied there was no imminent threat, we were allowed to go out of the reception building and across a road to the museum. Entry was only possible there, however, by scanning a QR code and making an online payment. Fortunately, we always seem to meet a friendly local person to help us out in these situations, and it was the same here. I think Ganesha puts them our way. After the kind chap ahead of us in the queue bought our tickets with his phone, we paid him back in cash and gave the man on the entrance to the museum some polite feedback on our user experience.

Spread over several galleries, the museum has an impressive portrait gallery and an extensive collection of coinage, weaponry, medals, and uniforms dating back to the colonial period. The architecture is a fascinating blend of British and Indian styles, with towering walls, grand arches, and sprawling courtyards that shout imperial might.

If anything symbolises the arrival of British power in India, it is Fort St George. When the East India Company came to India in the early 1600s, looking for spices, textiles, tea, indigo, opium… and anything else they could get their hands on, they soon realised they'd have to defend their foothold on the subcontinent. They needed a fort.

In 1639, the East India Company acquired a stretch of land next to present-day Marina Beach from the local Nayak rulers and set about building a defensive stronghold. The new fort was completed on 23 April 1644 (St George's Day) and dedicated to the patron saint of England. It was the first of many British forts, and they played significant roles in the East India Company's expansion and consolidation of power across India. Initially a modest trading post, the Fort Complex swiftly grew into a thriving city.

The East India Company was a remarkable entity. Established as a commercial trading company in 1600, it gradually developed to encompass a wide range of functions. It maintained a large private army, administered vast territories in India, and represented the interests of the British Crown. Over time, it became a major instrument of British colonial expansion and rule in India, wielding significant political and military power. The company's influence on the region's history, economy, and governance was profound, lasting until the British Crown assumed direct control of India in 1858.

Entering the museum building, it's impossible not to feel the immense historical significance of the fort. This is where so much about modern India first started. The first constabulary, hospital, mint, and other civic amenities were all established in the fort and became the template for development elsewhere in the country. Governor Sir William Langhorne has a lot to answer for. During his time in charge, from 1670 to 1678, he began the systematic filing of all transactions carried out at the fort. The information board at the museum tells us: 'A simple act, thus initiated, has become an obsession in the government offices in India today.' There you have it – this was the very birthplace of Indian bureaucracy!

When it comes to pointless red tape, things could have been worse; modern Indians should count themselves lucky that the French didn't hold on to power after briefly taking possession of the fort in 1746. The French had marched up from Pondicherry, seized the fort, and renamed it Fort Louis. However, 3 years later, they agreed to an exchange deal with England involving the French settlement of Louisbourg in North America. The East India Company then returned to Fort George to strengthen its defences and restore more practical levels of record management.

Robert Clive, famously known as 'Clive of India', had a significant and controversial association with the fort. He was first posted there when he joined the East India Company as a junior clerk in 1743. In maintaining the company's accounts and records, he played his own part in the systematic filing of transactions. His proclivity for systematic filling was later exceeded by a prowess for fighting. When the French captured Madras in 1746 during the War of the Austrian Succession, Clive escaped to Fort St David and volunteered to join the East India Company's military operations against the French. Clive's successful defence of Arcot in 1751 with a small force against a much larger French-led army established his reputation as a brilliant military leader and marked his transition from pen-pusher to soldier.

Robert Clive's legacy is marred by his role in the exploitation of India and his personal enrichment at the expense of the local population. When he returned to England in 1767, his wealth was estimated at around £401,102, which was an astronomical sum for the time – more than what some professional footballers earn each week today. Some estimates suggest that, in today's terms, Clive's wealth might be equivalent to around £7.5 billion. Despite a parliamentary inquiry and allegations of corruption and abuse of power, Clive had friends in high places and managed to retain much of his wealth and influence. While his military achievements are still recognised, his role in the exploitative practices of the East India Company and his personal enrichment at the expense of the Indian people are a shameful part of British colonial history. His legacy serves as a reminder of the darker aspects of the British Empire's presence in India.

On a lighter note, we saw in the museum what is claimed to be the oldest surviving Indian flag. Made of silk and measuring 3.5 metres by 2.4 metres, it was hoisted on the Fort St George flagstaff on India's first Independence Day, 15 August 1947, marking the end of British colonial rule. The flag's iconic tricolour design, with the Ashoka Chakra at its centre, embodies the values, aspirations, and identity of the Indian nation. The Ashoka Chakra, a navy-blue wheel with twenty-four spokes, represents virtues mentioned in Buddhist teachings and the cycle of life, death, and rebirth. Its circular motion symbolises the continuous progress of the nation and the forward movement of life. Now looking fragile, the flag is a priceless national treasure and a powerful symbol of India's freedom struggle.

Nick, Ellen, and I explored the fort complex and found our way to St Mary's Church, the oldest Anglican church in India. It was here that Robert Clive married Margaret Maskelyne on 18 February 1753. We tried to enter the historic building, but it was closed, which was both unfortunate and ironic since it was a Sunday. Wandering further, possibly through an army compound, we eventually found ourselves outside the fort complex, next to a huge roundabout with an impressive war memorial at its centre. We were told off by its guard for trying to get close enough to look at it, so we admired it from a distance. We took a tuk-tuk back to the restaurant we'd been to the previous day, and suddenly our time in India was almost up. The three of us returned to our hotel, packed, checked out, and headed for the airport.

We arrived earlier than expected and were initially turned away at the external security gate. Luckily, the nice soldier at the adjacent gate was more impressed by our pathetic tales of pensioner misfortune, and we managed to talk our way through. It meant we were able to find somewhere to sit during the long wait for our flight. With time to spare, we opted for mango milkshakes all around and took the opportunity to review our journey.

Hours later, as the plane took off from Chennai, I leaned back and closed my eyes, letting images from the past three weeks wash over me like a series of Instagram stories. From the bustling streets of Mumbai to the peaceful backwaters of Kerala, from the ancient temples of Hampi to the experimental township of Auroville, our journey through southern India had been a kaleidoscope of sights, sounds, and experiences.

The trip hadn't just been about ticking off bucket list items or collecting souvenirs, though we did plenty of both. We went to some crazy places. It was a chance to push ourselves out of our comfort zones and embrace the unknown. Through several challenges, frequent laughter, and several trouser-staining overtaking manoeuvres, we had seen many extraordinary sights and gained a better appreciation of the diversity of the human spirit. It also brought home the benefits of a robust spreadsheet, a phone battery pack, and a good medical kit.

India is different. Its endless contradictions and complexities reaffirmed valuable lessons about patience, adaptability, and the need for an open mind and heart. From the warmth and generosity of the people we met, to the confusing yet profound spiritual insights we discovered in places like Pune, Coimbatore, and Auroville, our journey had been a testament to the transformative power of travel – uncovering not just incredible places and people, but things about ourselves.

Our second adventure in India had left a reminder that life is to be lived fully, with courage, curiosity, gratitude, travel insurance, and a sense of adventure… we certainly tried to embrace that spirit.

To all fellow travellers, young and old, especially those wondering if they can take on such a trip: embrace the journey, wherever it takes you. Let yourself be challenged and inspired by the wonders of the world. It's never too late to embark on the adventure of a lifetime. Where will you go?

REFLECTIONS

Looking back on our *Journey through Southern India* several months after returning home, those final thoughts from Chennai still sum up the journey quite well. What lingers in my mind are not just the awe-inspiring sights we saw, the curries we enjoyed, or the miles we covered, but the experiences that shaped our journey and the generosity of the people we met.

Travel is partly about visiting extraordinary places, and in our two adventures across India (the first was in 2020), Nick and I certainly did that. Among the many iconic sights we encountered, some were unique to India – you can't see the Taj Mahal anywhere else.

If I was reading a travel memoir, I would want to know which places had made the biggest impact on the author, so as I'm a bloke and I don't need much encouragement to make a list, I've put together my top ten sights from eight weeks travel over two trips. Half of these are UNESCO World Heritage Sites:

1. The Taj Mahal – an exquisite masterpiece of Mughal architecture that is so perfect, it's hard to believe it could have been produced by the hand of man. The impeccably balanced iconic white marble, with its intricate inlay of precious stones, lived up to its reputation, taking my breath away as it emerged from the mist on the banks of the Yamuna River. Renowned for its symmetry and timeless beauty, the Taj Mahal is one of those 'you have to be there' places. It surpassed my expectations. Don't even think about it – go.

2. Varanasi – one of the oldest continuously inhabited cities in the world, Varanasi is possibly the most remarkable place I've ever visited. Its sacred atmosphere envelops you as you mingle with orange-clad pilgrims, ash-covered sadhus, and the timeless rituals of cremation and prayer on the banks of the holy Ganges River. It's raw, visceral, and profoundly moving.

3. The Kailasa Temple, Ellora – labelled by British archaeologists in the 19th century as simply 'Cave 16,' this temple is an extraordinary feat of engineering, devotion, and artistry. Carved from a single rock, it is the largest monolithic structure in the world and represents Mount Kailash, the mythical abode of Lord Shiva. The sheer precision and scale, achieved without modern tools, make it one of the most awe-inspiring architectural achievements in human history.

4. Hampi – once the capital of the Vijayanagara Empire and the second-largest city in the world, Hampi's landscape of ancient ruins, grand temples, and surreal boulder-strewn terrain is unforgettable. Its rich history, featuring Hindu legends and cultural brilliance, left an indelible impression on me – especially as we were there during the festival of Diwali. It's one of the most remarkable and evocative historical sites in India.

5. Amritsar – the Golden Temple in Amritsar, with its gold-covered sanctum surrounded by a shimmering water tank, is the holiest site in Sikhism and a masterpiece of spiritual and architectural brilliance. The city's colonial history, marked by the Jallianwala Bagh massacre, adds a poignant layer to its significance. The temple is not just a symbol of resilience and devotion, but also a place that echoes India's struggles and triumphs.

6. The beaches of Goa – even during our very brief visit, it was clear that Goa's golden sands and swaying palms are the perfect place to unwind. Those beaches, once a haven for hippies, now blend Portuguese colonial influence with a modern wellness vibe, offering yoga retreats and tranquil escapes. I found myself wanting to stay longer, and I want to be there now.

7. The Thar Desert – I will always remember sleeping under the stars in the Thar Desert. The sheer expanse of the night sky and the stillness of the desert left me in silent awe. Nick and I lay there with nothing but the open desert around us, and billions of stars overhead. It was a simple but profound reminder of the vastness of the universe and our small place within it.

8. Shimla – literally a cool, refreshing breath of fresh air, Shimla is nestled in the serene Himalayan foothills, surrounded by dense pine forests and vibrant rhododendrons. Winding mountain roads lead you to remnants of colonial England, with the magnificent Viceregal Lodge reminding you that this was once the summer retreat of the powerful British Raj. The quaint toy train, bustling bazaars, and stunning sunsets over the towering Himalayas make this a very special place indeed.

9. Adiyogi Shiva, Coimbatore – standing 112 feet tall, the Adiyogi Shiva statue is a breathtaking monument designed to symbolise the source of yoga. Witnessing the evening light show, with the shadowy Western Ghats in the background, created a nerve-tingling experience blending spirituality, artistry, and a deep connection to India's ancient wisdom.

10. Tea plantations, Munnar – rolling emerald-green tea plantations blanket the mist-covered hills of Munnar, offering a cool and tranquil escape from the heat and chaos of India's cities. This breathtaking landscape, steeped in history and framed by the Western Ghats, offers a heady mixture of natural and man-made beauty.

These were the highlights, from a long list of extraordinary places that Nick and I sought out, far from the comfortable surroundings and routines of our normal daily lives. Seasoned travellers like Nick and me still react like a couple of excited schoolboys on journeys like these. We still retain a sense of wonder, an urge to see what's around the next corner, and a willingness to be inspired. Travelling through India allowed us, for a brief while, to escape the ordinary – to think beyond the next trip to the supermarket, renewing the TV licence, or worrying about the next energy supplier switch.

While these jaw-dropping sights and so many others during our two trips – like Mysore Palace, Auroville and Rajasthan – were unforgettable, it was often the lesser-known places that had the most profound impact. And there were plenty of them across an incredible range of landscapes and habitats. Being the seventh largest country in the world, India has a vast array of ecosystems, ranging from alpine (Shimla) to tropical (Goa), desert (Jaisalmer) to coastal (Puducherry). Balancing that complexity, India keeps things simple for us English speakers by allowing us to converse in our native tongue in many places, by only having one time zone and driving on the left (mostly).

Thats the *place*, but India is so much more of course. It has immense religious and spiritual significance, for example. It is the birthplace of four major world religions: Hinduism, Buddhism, Jainism, and Sikhism, all of which have shaped society for millennia. Hindus make up nearly 80% of the population, Muslims account for around 14%, Christians for approximately 2.3%, and followers of other faiths like Sikhism, Buddhism, and Jainism together represent around 4% of the population. It makes India a diverse and deeply spiritual nation and whether you go looking for it or not, travelling in India envelopes you in a rich spiritual experience where ancient temples, daily rituals, and sacred sites slowly impress upon you the depth of the country's long-standing traditions and beliefs.

As of 2024, India is the fifth-largest economy in the world and economic forecasts indicate that by 2030, it will become the third largest. The cultural and religious backdrop, briefly mentioned above, including the influence of various colonial powers, has benefited some sectors of society more than others, resulting in a population and economy of contrasting fortunes and extremes. And that enormous economic pie has to be shared by the most populous country in the world. With India's nominal GDP per capita coming in at 129th in the world, for some, that economic pie is barely crumbs. In Mumbai, it's possible to find a billionaire and a beggar sharing the same pavement – a snapshot of the city's, and the country's, striking socio-economic disparities. The same country that nurtures the centuries-old Kathakali dance tradition is also pioneering 21st-century space exploration, with successful missions to Mars and the Moon's south pole. This blend of the ancient and the modern, rich and poor, the traditional and the innovative, makes India mysterious, unpredictable and fascinating.

India's people, with their warmth, resilience, and generosity, have left a lasting impression, reinforcing that travel is as much about human connections as it is about the places we visit. That unexpected invitation to a puja, the countless unprompted huge smiles from our tuk-tuk drivers, and the offers of help and support from complete strangers – they meant so much more to us than those people will ever know. These memories serve as a reminder of the privilege of travel, a gift that not everyone is fortunate enough to experience. And for travellers like Nick and me, approaching middle age, these journeys have generated experiences that will last long after returning home.

For so many reasons, my *Journey through Southern India* will stay with me, as long as the memory holds out, inspiring future travel and adventures. As I navigate my eighth decade, it has proven that, with the blessing of good health, age is no barrier to exploration – and, if old duffers like Nick and me can do it, so can you. There is an immediate 'in the moment' enjoyment from the thrill of an adventure like ours, but the deeper benefit is how it changes us over time – making us more aware, more understanding, and more appreciative of the world's many wonders. In Pune, Coimbatore, Mysuru, and Puducherry, we came face to face with some of those 'big questions of existence' I mentioned in the opening chapter of this book. Those encounters, combined with experiences in places like Amritsar, Bodh Gaya, and Varanasi on our previous trip, have provided me with plenty of thoughtful reflection.

Over the last few years, my interest in yoga has led me to explore the roots and development of that ancient philosophy and holistic practice. For me, that has opened up many intriguing connections to health, wellbeing, spirituality, and awareness. I might just have to return to India to explore those issues further…

ACKNOWLEDGEMENTS

Once again, I find myself indebted to so many people who enabled me to complete my *Journey through Southern India*, helping me to turn my rambling account into my fourth published book. This is the first of my books that is not self-published. I am deeply grateful to Adrian Phillips, Hugh Brune, Anna Moores, Claire Strange, and all the team at Bradt for their friendly support and professional guidance along the path to publication with them.

As always, I shared every step, every biryani, every 'heart in the mouth' overtaking manoeuvre, and every lost laundry bag with my great pal, Nick Lindsay. I couldn't wish for a better friend to accompany me through thick and thin. I'm incredibly lucky, and as I've said before: everyone should have a friend like Nick. It was also a real pleasure to share the final part of our trip with Nick's wife, Ellen, who brought much-needed decorum and a welcome sense of order to our adventures. That's probably how we managed to get home again.

This journey would not have been the same without the incredible hospitality and warmth we encountered throughout India. To the owners and managers of the many hotels, hostels, B&Bs — and not forgetting the houseboat — we extend our deepest thanks. The kindness of so many Indian people who welcomed us, befriended us, and even insisted on sharing their phone numbers in case we needed help is something we will long remember.

To the fearless tuk-tuk, taxi, and bus drivers who navigated us, sometimes safely, through the bustling streets and main roads of

ACKNOWLEDGEMENTS

India, thank you for somehow delivering us in one piece! And to Ganesha, whether or not he was truly guiding our journey, we owe a nod for any divine intervention he provided along the way.

A heartfelt thank-you to Jill Sawyer for her exceptional editing skills and patience; her magic touch transformed my sprawling manuscript into something readable. Tom Probert's creativity shines through in another beautiful cover — a true masterpiece, as always. I'm very happy for people to judge this book by its cover.

I'm also very grateful to my yoga teacher, Lisa Wylde, who made the meeting with Prashant Iyengar possible and reviewed my description of yoga.

Finally, and most importantly, my deepest gratitude and love go to Jan, who continues to tolerate a husband prone to wanderlust who frequently 'goes off to do silly things'. Your patience and support mean more to me than I could ever put into words.

ABOUT MARK PROBERT

Mark Probert has spent most of his life as a mapmaker. His early career with OS, the national mapping agency, allowed him to travel widely in Britain. He set up his own company in 2003 and over the following 16 years, he travelled extensively overseas, working on five continents. Now retired, and living in rural Dorset, he spends his time writing, walking, cycling, and motorcycling. Mark and Jan have a daughter, two sons, and a granddaughter.

Mark published his first book in 2020. In *Another Journey through Britain*, he uses gentle humour to describe a two-week motorcycle ride through the back lanes of Britain. Along the way, Mark compares what he comes across with the Britain of 50 years ago, as described in the book *Journey through Britain*, written by John Hillaby. Mark published *Journey through India* in 2021 and followed up with *Journey through Wales* in 2022.

To catch up with Mark's latest writing, view his gallery of images, and purchase his other books, please visit his website at mgprobert.com.

ABOUT NICK LINDSAY

Born in Cardiff in 1957, Nick Lindsay began his working life with Ordnance Survey, the national mapping agency of Great Britain. He left in 1980 to continue his education with a degree, followed by a PhD in geology at the University of Liverpool. Employment as a geologist gave him the chance to travel extensively. Now retired and living in the Highlands, he spends his time as chairman of Clyne Heritage Society, running, writing, and walking in his beloved Scottish mountains. Nick is married to Ellen, and they share their house with four cats.

Nick published his first book in 2010, *Cape Wrath to Brora: A walking adventure across Sutherland*. His second book, *Clyne, Loth & Golspie place names*, was published in 2016, and his third, a biography of a larger-than-life character from Doll: *We had nothing, but we had everything: George MacBeath's memories of growing up on a croft, at Doll, Brora*, was published in 2020.

Other Mark Probert titles on Amazon

"A light-hearted motorcycle road trip through the back lanes of Great Britain."

"Two pensioners backpack their way across the subcontinent... what could go wrong?"

"A summer road trip of discovery and smiles."

'Take everything you like seriously, except yourselves.'
Rudyard Kipling